10.00

D1293180

A Time in Arabia

A Time in Arabia

DOREEN INGRAMS

JOHN MURRAY

Printed in Great Britain by
Cox & Wyman Ltd., London Fakenham
and Reading

0 7195 2050 9

To the men and women
of the Hadhramaut

'When you break bread with people and share their troubles and joys, the barriers of language, of politics and of religion soon vanish.'

JULIEN BRYAN

CONTENTS

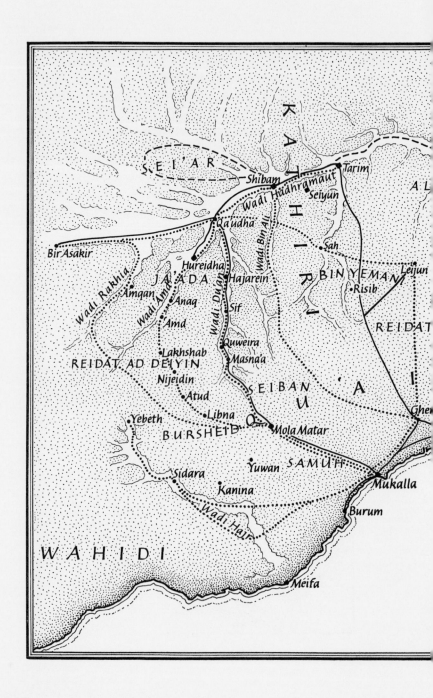

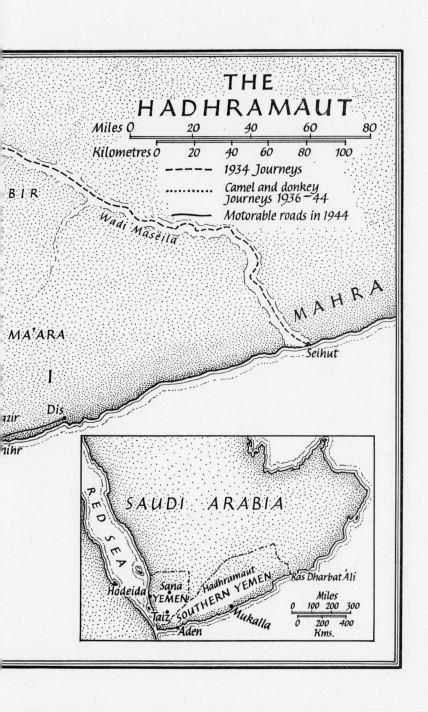

THE
HADHRAMAUT

Miles 0   20   40   60   80

Kilometres 0   20   40   60   80   100

- - - - - 1934 Journeys

·········· Camel and donkey
Journeys 1936–44

——— Motorable roads in 1944

B I R

Wadi Maseila

MA'ARA

MAHRA

I

Seihut

Dis

azir

uhr

RED SEA

SAUDI ARABIA

Hodeida

Sana
YEMEN

Hadhramaut

Rás Dharbat Áli

Taiz SOUTHERN YEMEN

Mukalla

Aden

Miles
0   100 200 300

0   200   400
Kms.

ILLUSTRATIONS

*All photographs are the author's
except where otherwise acknowledged*

ILLUSTRATIONS

FOREWORD

During the years that I lived in the Hadhramaut I kept a diary. It was the first time that Europeans had ever made a home in that country and at first each day's entries took up many pages, but gradually there were only unusual events to record for what had seemed strange at first had become commonplace. It is these diaries that are the basis of this book.

The account of journeys by camel or donkey thirty years ago may seem as archaic as the wagon trains of the wild west, yet there are still many parts of South Arabia which can only be visited by camel, although the aeroplane and the motor-car have brought many towns closer together. I revisited the country in 1963 covering by air much of the area that I had plodded over and I reflected how fortunate I had been to have had the chance of that slow motion view, since no one can appreciate how people live by a bird's eye view of a country, or the isolation of airport or hotel.

It was my good fortune also to spend much of the time with the women, in particular with the Al Kaf family whose kindness it would be impossible to exaggerate. Because I owed them so much – their friendship, their help, and their hospitality, I hesitated for years to write about the life behind their front doors as it seemed an intolerable abuse of hospitality. Now, however, many years have gone by and I would like others to share the enjoyment and the interest I found among them and among the women in many different parts of the Hadhramaut. I would not like to offend and anything I write about my friends is written in appreciation of their courage in the face of suffering, of their patience in a frustrating life, and of the kindly way they welcomed me into their homes.

ACKNOWLEDGEMENTS

I would like to thank both family and friends, especially Jane Boulenger, for their criticism and advice.

Chapter One

INTRODUCTION TO SOUTH ARABIA

'My country is my country, even if it be a barren rock' is an Arab saying that probably applies nowhere more aptly than to South Arabia, known today as the People's Republic of Southern Yemen. The change of name may have made that area of the Arabian Peninsula sound united but behind it lie the same disunited tribal states that once formed the Aden Protectorate.

The British had ruled Aden as a colony, and had subsequently controlled the hinterland as a protectorate, since the 19th January 1839 when Captain Stafford Bettesworth Haines of the British Navy captured Aden in the name of Her Majesty Queen Victoria from the Sultan of Lahej, whose capital lay some miles to the north. Captain Haines not only laid the foundations for the growth of Aden into a flourishing commercial centre, important port, and strategic base, but he entered into the first treaties with tribal chiefs in the vicinity of Aden, paying them stipends and offering them the protecting power of Her Majesty's Government in order to have their good will and prevent them interfering in the development of the colony of Aden. Over the years as one British Resident succeeded another more treaties were made with more tribal chiefs, until by the twentieth century the Aden Protectorate appeared on the maps as an area covering about 112,000 square miles surrounded by the protective red of the British Empire. There were over twenty tribal states in treaty relations, varying in size from a village to a state the size of Wales, and the chiefs were entitled to stipends and to seven or more gun salutes according to the importance of their territories which, in most cases, were only nominally under their control.

Looking down on South Arabia from the air it appears as uninviting as the moon, a jagged succession of mountains cut

by ravines, or flat empty spaces of sand or stone. No water
and scarcely any cultivation can be seen and it is impossible
to believe that man can survive on such barren land. But
cross those same flat empty spaces on a camel, or clamber
down the mountain passes on foot to the valleys, and you
meet men and women to whom 'my country is my country
even if it be a barren rock' is as full of meaning as 'England's
green and pleasant land' is to those who live in that island.

The South Arabian who survives the hazards of birth and
infancy becomes self-sufficient, fierce to defend such property
as he owns, suspicious of strangers, yet hospitable as only
desert dwellers who appreciate the value of food and water
can be hospitable, and with an innate pride in belonging to
the Arab race and in being a follower in the footsteps of
Muhammad. This feeling of Arab-ness and Muslim brotherhood is not confined to the beduin tribesman but is to be
found in the offices and trading centres of Aden as much as in
the mountain villages, and it explains why anything that
affects an Arab anywhere affects Arabs everywhere. Palestine
may be far away from South Arabia measured in miles but to
the South Arabian Palestine is as much a part of the Arab
homeland as is his own particular corner of it. This unity of
Arab-ness does not mean unity of thought, word and deed,
for the feuds and revolutions of South Arabia and the bitter
quarrels of the greater Arab powers show that underlying
that unity is the natural individualism of man, whether he
lives in an Arab country or in the mountains of Scotland or
Wales.

When a tribesman from the hinterland came to Aden
during the time of British rule he had to leave his gun at a
police post, a sign that he was not only entering a detribalized
world but the orderly world of a British colony, far removed
from the chaotic tribal life of the protected states. Until 1937
Aden itself was not in fact administered by the Colonial
Office but by the Government of India, as it was then called,
The Protectorate, however, had come into the orbit of the
Colonial Office a few years earlier and so Harold, who was a
member of the Colonial Service, was able to achieve his long

awaited objective of serving in South Arabia. He was appointed Political Officer in the Aden Protectorate by the Colonial Office but served under the Resident of Aden, who wore two hats, one which as chief executive officer of Aden he lifted to the Government of India, the other which as officer in charge of the Protectorate he took off to the Colonial Office. In 1937 he was relieved of one hat and was left with just the plumed cocked hat of a colonial governor. Thirty years ago these ceremonial hats seemed likely to sit on the heads of colonial governors for as long as could be foreseen by those who wore them.

The influence of the Government of India lay heavy upon Aden with its ugly, unimaginative government offices and official houses, and the innumerable Indian clerks, traders, police officers and schoolmasters who, through no fault of theirs as it was the Government of India that gave them their jobs, delayed the opportunities for the native born Adeni to take their place.

The Indian connection struck us soon after we arrived in Aden by the Peninsula and Orient Line ship on 1st April 1934. The Resident, Colonel (afterwards Sir Bernard) Reilly had invited us to stay and having come ashore early in the morning we sat down to breakfast with him and his A.D.C. As it was Sunday we were served mulligatawny soup and rice. That was not the only Sunday ritual, the P. & O. Line ships arrived regularly each Sunday morning and on being sighted a gun was fired to let all the homesick expatriates know that their mail was on the way and could be collected from the Post Office in an hour or so. Although the servants were nearly all Arabs from the hinterland they were expected to cast aside their *futas* (short skirts) and put on white trousers, long white coats and red turbans like an Indian *khitmagar*. They became proficient in using Anglo-Indian jargon, *chota hazri, chota peg, sahib* and – to my horror – *memsahib*, a name which even in those far off days conjured up to me the worst type of British woman abroad. The fact that I had a rather unconventional approach to life in a colony may have been partly the result of having been on the stage in the days when

touring showed you a world of 'digs', slum life and mixing
with anybody and everybody, all far removed from the protective shell of my parents' home. But I had also married a
man with an independent mind who refused to conform to the
mystique of the British in the colonies, the social round that
excluded 'natives', the formalities of calling, dress, and way of
talking to the 'lesser breeds', all of which were supposedly
keeping up British prestige, or so I was assured on the occa-
sions when I questioned British behaviour.

We settled in an eyrie on a hilltop in the unfashionable part
of Aden known as Crater, surrounded by lava-strewn hills, a
decision which was thought somewhat eccentric, although
Crater was in fact the mercantile centre where all the real life
of Aden was to be found. Newcomers to the British colony put
up a box at their front door, and those amongst the old
British community who thought they would call on you did so
by leaving their cards in the box, then, after a suitable lapse
of time, the newcomers reversed the process. Having raised
your hats, so to speak, to each other the newcomer then
waited for an invitation to a cocktail party or a meal. There
was also the even more important ritual of writing your name
in the Resident's book, if this were not done you would be
unlikely to receive an invitation to the Residency.

Water was rationed and there was not a W.C. anywhere;
even after grand dinners at the Residency the ladies retired
from the table to share a 'thunderbox', a commode emptied
by sweepers who were the lowest form of human life. Arabs do
not have the caste system of Hindus but there are divisions in
society nevertheless. A tribesman might be prepared to earn
money by working for a European as a servant, equal to
his master and definitely superior to his mistress, but he
would never dream of doing the menial work which a
poor man with no tribal attachments was prepared to
undertake.

Harold went off every morning to an uninspiring building
in Steamer Point known as the Secretariat where he sat day
after day dealing with tribal affairs, which amounted to
little more than deciding which chief should have more arms

and which should not, or who was deserving of an increased stipend, or what section of what tribe was causing trouble on a caravan route. Meanwhile as we had Zaidi from Zanzibar, who had been with Harold for many years, looking after the house, and Ganess of Mauritius cooking our meals, I felt a need to have some interest also and asked a young Arab to give me conversation lessons; the crash course Harold and I had taken in Arabic at the School of Oriental Languages had given us a good grounding in Arabic grammar but had not prepared us for the Adeni dialect.

Ahmed and I talked together and read the Quran, when he would put on his tarbush, put out his cigarette, and be careful that the Book should not be touched except with clean hands nor laid aside under any other book. He was a very thoughtful, amiable man who was working as a dispenser and it was through him that I made my first contact with the Ali Jaffers, an Arab family, who were well known in Aden for supplying responsible, loyal civil servants. Ahmed told me he had three aunts he would like me to visit, and as we walked to his home I pictured the sort of elderly women I was to meet, but they turned out to be three charming young girls, half sisters to Ahmed's father Ibrahim who introduced me to Fakhria, Qadria and Rahima with the words 'They are all virgins'. The family was Persian in origin and of the Shia sect, which meant that the girls could not marry a local Arab Sunni but had to be allotted a relative from the extensive Jaffer family or from its relatives the Hasanalis; not quite extensive enough, however, for there were no husbands for these three who faced a life of spinsterhood, an unhappy state in a society where practically every girl married and where there was at that time no possibility of a career for them. Fakhria, the eldest, remained at home, but Qadria many years later became a sewing teacher at the girls' school in Aden, earning her own living and a measure of freedom, whilst Rahima, the youngest, eventually took up assistant nursing in England. She was always the adventurous one, filled with an urge to leave her restricted surroundings and see the world, and her adventures began when she came to

B

live with us in the Hadhramaut – but that lay several years ahead.

It was not long before Harold grew impatient with his unproductive work at the Secretariat, and after some short trips into tribal areas near Aden to sort out various problems, he convinced the Resident of the need to visit the little known, distant Hadhramaut in the eastern part of the Aden Protectorate, in order to examine the political, social and economic conditions of the two states in that area, the Qu'aiti State of Shihr and Mukalla and the Kathiri State of Seiyun.

Hadhramaut means 'death is present' and for the most part the country lives up to its name: it is largely desert and the people have to scratch a living from the few places where agriculture is possible, in the valleys or along the coastal plains. It is not a desert of sand, except in the northernmost areas that border the Empty Quarter, but a desert of stones which stretches for mile after mile on the *jols*, or plateaux, that lie between the coastal hills and the Wadi Hadhramaut, the great valley that cuts through the country from north west to south east. This landscape may not sound very attractive, and indeed, many people found the stark nakedness of Hadhramaut *jols* repelling, but to me they always held the fascination of emptiness stretching to the horizon, of changing lights, and of the increased awareness of every boulder or stunted shrub. There was, too, the added enhancement that the brown *jols* gave to the green of the wadis which suddenly opened to view from the steep passes leading down to them. A *wadi* can be translated as a valley, a river valley, a gorge, a ravine, or just a river; in the Hadhramaut a wadi could be from a few hundred yards to several miles wide. It might have cultivated plots of land, date palms, numerous villages, or it might just be a stretch of sand and boulders. Somewhere winding tortuously through a wadi there was always a dried up river-bed, covered with stones and scrub, never cultivated because when the flood waters came pouring down the ravines leading from the *jols* they followed the river-bed, sweeping everything before them. The villages were built on the sides of the wadis above the flood waters and the cultivators built small dams to try and save some of the precious water that was largely lost in the sea to the south or in the sandy wastes to the north.

The Qu'aiti State of Shihr and Mukalla extends for some 200 miles along the coast of South Arabia and some 150 miles inland, whilst the Kathiri State forms an enclave in the north with no outlet to the sea. The capital of the Qu'aiti State is the port of Mukalla, and it has several other important towns, notably Shibam, famed for its 'skyscrapers', which lies in Wadi Hadhramaut over a hundred miles north of Mukalla. There are two important towns in the Kathiri State, Seiyun the capital, and Tarim. Both are in Wadi Hadhramaut and lie to the east of Shibam. At the time of our first visit to the country in 1934 the Qu'aiti and Kathiri Sultans had only nominal control of the areas outside these towns.

Any estimate of the population of the two states would be guesswork as there has never been a census, but it may perhaps be 200,000 to 300,000. There are many difficulties in trying to estimate the size of a population without a proper census, something that was impossible to carry out as it would have caused uproar among the tribesmen who would have assumed it was a prelude to further taxation. To try to obtain some idea of the population, Harold and I asked about the number of armed men in each tribe or clan, and when riding through villages, from the advantageous height of a camel's hump, I would assess how many huts there were, estimate four people to a hut and conclude that the population of that village was X number of huts multiplied by four. Not a very accurate census.

The bulk of the people of the Hadhramaut are tribesmen, living in settlements or nomadic but there are several other 'classes' – townsmen, agricultural labourers, slaves, and seiyids. These last can be described as the titled people, as seiyid is a title given to the descendants of the prophet Muhammad. The seiyids in the Hadhramaut were to be found in their greatest number in the Kathiri State where many of them were extremely wealthy and exercised much influence on the lives of the people. Even the poorest seiyid was respected for his ancestry and was expected to arbitrate in tribal feuds.

The difficulty of making a living from the largely desert country of the Hadhramaut had for many years caused numbers of Hadhramis to emigrate in order to support their families by remittances from wherever they had gone to seek a living, in Java, Singapore, Hyderabad or East Africa. As might be expected the tendency was for the men from one area to favour, say, East Africa, while from another they would all flock to Singapore, and from yet another to Hyderabad, but as soon as they had saved money they returned to their beloved homeland.

In 1934 there was no organised government in either the Qu'aiti or Kathiri states and the Sultans 'ruled' more or less personally with the aid of a secretary, a treasurer, a judge, and a commander of the forces. In the Qu'aiti State the forces were quite impressive, there was a police force in Mukalla and an army of some 700 men recruited from Yafa'i tribesmen or from slaves, the two sections of the population likely to be most loyal – the Yafa'is because, although they were not actually Hadhramis at all, they had an interest in the country as the Qu'aiti Sultans originated from Yafa'i, and the slaves because their bread and butter depended upon their loyalty. The Kathiri State had no organized force but bands of armed retainers loyal to the Sultan.

Slaves formed an important class in the community. Their fathers or grandfathers had originally come from Africa and we still came across occasional attempts at slave trading among dhow captains who sailed between East Africa and South Arabia, but the slave trade had been made illegal long before we first saw the Hadhramaut. Slavery, however, existed legally until 1937 when Harold advised the Sultans to offer manumission to those who wanted it. There were many Hadhramis who were called slaves but who had in fact been freed; they were black, looked more African than Arab, and consequently were always referred to in Arabic as *abid* or slaves. Children of slaves remained slaves, but children of a free father and slave mother were free as they took their status from their father. No free girl would be allowed to marry a slave, in fact permissiveness in matrimony was a good guide to class distinctions, for while a man could marry anyone of his own class or lower, a girl could only marry a man of her own class or higher. Thus a *sherifa* (the title given to a female descendant of the Prophet) could only marry a seiyid as they were the 'Top People', but a tribeswoman had the choice of a tribesman or a seiyid, but could not marry an agricultural labourer. At the bottom of the scale came, not the slaves, but the Subians who did the menial work such as clearing out the 'thunderboxes' of Aden or the 'long drops' of the Hadhramaut.

Our first visit to the Hadhramaut in 1934–35 lasted nine weeks, during which time we covered a great deal of ground, literally as well as figuratively. From Mukalla we went by donkey to Wadi Hadhramaut via Wadi Du'an, then into the northern tribal areas, back to the Wadi Hadhramaut to stay for a time in Shibam and Tarim, then on camels along the length of the wadi to the sea at Seihut, the first time Europeans had taken this route. Wherever we went we had to take a protector from the tribe through whose territory we wanted to pass as the whole country was bedevilled by tribal feuds, and without such protection we and the beduins with us might well have been shot. On one occasion, even when we had a protector, there was a long altercation with tribesmen who did not consider protection should cover Christians.

We found out as much as we could about the tribal organisation, the economy of the country, and the social conditions, and we mapped a good deal of hitherto unmapped territory, all of which was published in Harold's official *Colonial Report No. 123* and then later in his book *Arabia and the Isles*, but although we had covered so much we had only skimmed the surface of the life of the people, and it was not until the Hadhramaut became our home that we could begin to appreciate the Hadhrami.

Chapter Two

RETURN TO THE HADHRAMAUT

After the publication of Harold's official report on conditions in the Hadhramaut the British Government decided that further investigation should be made to see if it were feasible to aid the Qu'aiti and Kathiri Sultans in developing their states. It had become clear that there were influential leaders in the Hadhramaut who were asking 'What is the use of a Protectorate treaty if the protecting power takes no interest in those it is protecting?'

The Protectorate treaties extended His Majesty's Government's protection to the rulers in South Arabia who, for their part, undertook not to correspond or have treaty relations with any other foreign power, but there was to be no interference in the internal affairs of the states unless caravan routes to Aden were disrupted by tribal wars. This policy of non-interference worked reasonably well in the western part of the Aden Protectorate where most of the tribes made it abundantly clear that they neither wanted advice, direction nor control of any kind, but it was a different matter in the Hadhramaut where a large and important section of the population had prospered in well-ordered countries such as Java and Singapore and were anxious to have peace and better administration in their own country. In the autumn of 1936 Harold returned to the Hadhramaut to find out how help could best be given, what such help would involve and, of importance to the British taxpayer, what it was likely to cost.

We arrived back in Mukalla in November 1936, almost two years to the day of our first visit, and it all seemed much the same as we drove from the quayside through the main street to the guest house; the sights and smells had not changed, but there was in fact a difference, a new Qu'aiti Sultan of Shihr and Mukalla had succeeded, bringing with him new personalities in positions of power.

The Qu'aiti dynasty had been founded by a successful leader of mercenaries from the Yafa'i tribe, whose territory lies to the west of the Hadhramaut, who had been called in by a Hadhrami Sultan to help fight his enemies. He found, like many rulers before him, that the mercenaries took over and ousted him. The first Qu'aiti Sultan laid it down that succession should go from brother to brother, then back to first brother's son, over to his cousin, and so on. This was a direct encouragement to each Sultan to make as much as he could while in power in order to safeguard the interests of his children who would not benefit again until the other branch of the family had had a go. This situation was further complicated because the Qu'aitis had been accustomed to emigrate to Hyderabad and the Sultans of Shihr and Mukalla were also Jemadars, or officers, in the Nizam's army, with considerable estates in Hyderabad. They spent as much, if not more, time looking after their interests in India as they spent looking after their State of Shihr and Mukalla.

The new Sultan, Salih bin Ghalib, unlike many of his predecessors really took an interest in his South Arabian state, but when he first became Sultan he knew little about the country as he had spent most of his life in Hyderabad. He was not a young man when he succeeded and I remember I was not impressed the first time I saw him, lumbering heavily out of his car backwards, his huge body encased in Indian-style long coat and tight trousers, a fez on the top of his small head, moving slowly among the people assembled to meet him, raising his hand wearily to his forehead, over and over again, in an informal acknowledgement of their greetings. His pallid face gave him a sickly appearance. He rarely smiled, but when he did there was no mistaking the sincerity and kindliness that were hidden behind his unprepossessing exterior. He disliked the intrigue that he knew was going on around him, for he was a straightforward man who liked to get down to practical issues, avoiding wherever possible the distasteful jealousies and clash of personalities among those who were nearest to him. His interests and hobbies were unexpected and ranged from photography and geology to electricity; anything mechanical fascinated him and when he had an engine installed in the royal dhow it was that which occupied his attention when he went visiting coastal towns rather than the petty disputes he had gone to settle. He wanted to utilize all the resources of his state for the benefit of his people by developing fishing and agriculture, or by investigating the mineral resources, including oil. Much of this became known to us later when he had given his full support and confidence to Harold, but from the first day of meeting him and talking to him we appreciated his genuine concern for the state he had only recently acquired.

Sultan Salih had two wives but neither of them shared his palace in Mukalla. His Number One wife was a first cousin whom he had married when very young and who lived on the top floor of the old palace, a high building near the harbour. She was much respected for her piety, held court surrounded by attendant slaves, and was visited by her husband on feast days. Sultan Salih's other wife remained in India and was the mother of his only surviving child, a son called Awadh, who was later made heir apparent by a change in the Qu'aiti dynastic law and subsequently became Sultan. Awadh was always sickly and died in early middle age to be succeeded by his son Ghalib, called from his school in England to take up his position as ruler. Ghalib was only Sultan for a year or so before being deposed when the Republic of Southern Yemen was proclaimed in 1967.

We had not long been settled into the guest house in Mukalla before we became aware of the intrigues between different factions, made more striking by the fact that it was Ramadhan when social contacts take place at night, and the mysterious comings and goings of political favourites and cast-out favourites had the atmosphere of a Tudor court. The two outstanding personalities, against whom Harold continually received complaints, were Seiyid Hamid al Mihdhar, the *Wazir* or Minister, and Ahmed Nasir al Batati, commander of the state forces. I am not sure how it was that Seiyid Hamid had ingratiated himself into favour but he was from Wadi Du'an, a province to the north-west of Mukalla,

and he did his best to ensure preferential treatment for his
fellow Du'anis, while his co-favourite, Ahmed Nasir, saw to
it that he and his relatives reaped substantial benefit from
his position not only as commander of the forces but as a man
with considerable mercantile interests. Of the two I much
preferred Ahmed Nasir who could 'smile and smile and be a
villain'. He was very tall, good-looking, with a great sense of
humour and a sure eye for the main chance, which in the end
made him a loyal and trusted friend to Harold. Seiyid
Hamid, on the other hand, was a smooth, oily character,
outwardly jovial but with unsmiling eyes, and when eventually fortune went against him he disappeared to his remote
village.

After a week or two in Mukalla for Harold to assess the
situation and to have talks with the Sultan, we set off up-
country for the Kathiri State, travelling by the eastern route
from the port of Shihr up to Tarim in Wadi Hadhramaut. To
reach Shihr we drove eastwards by car along the golden
sands that stretch for mile after mile, leaving Mukalla at an
hour when the tide was low, so that we might drive at speed
on the hard packed sand, scattering yellow crabs in all directions. They had an instinctive road sense and always got out
of the way in the nick of time, and were fascinating creatures,
full of curiosity; they would come to inspect you, or pinch
your toes, if you lay on the beach, and were tiresomely acquis-
itive for they would steal anything small enough to take to
their underground homes. They were, however, fastidious as
I remember Harold testing one by putting a cigarette stub
down a hole, at once up came an indignant crab waving it in
the air to deposit the unpleasant object well away from his
front door.

Shihr had once been as important a port as Mukalla but it
was now little more than a fishing village and the only building of any size was the old whitewashed, crumbling-walled,
palace where we stayed with the governor, a friendly man
who tried unsuccessfully to hide his grey hairs with applica-
tions of henna, and who was addicted to betel chewing so that
wherever he went a servant followed carrying a spitoon to

catch the chewed up leaves. He was very considerate to his guests at meals, throwing over a choice piece of meat or holding out a titbit in his grubby fingers, and I have never heard anyone who could belch so loudly.

We took a walk round Shihr in the early morning followed by a large crowd. Later on I became accustomed to go out sightseeing only to find that I myself was the sight, with crowds of small boys getting under my feet, stirring up the dust, and people pushing and jostling each other to get a closer look at me. In spite of the noisy crowds Shihr had a charm of its own in its apparent indifference to the outside world, content to make a living from the sea. There had been heavy rain during the night which had left puddles everywhere and which brought delight to the inhabitants, who had the additional excitement of two unusual strangers. Drawn to the beach by the sound of chanting, we watched a group of fishermen hauling in nets full of small fish, rhythmically singing of their catch with each tug. As the nets were emptied the fish piled up into heaps of shimmering silver, glittering in the sun and flapping out their last breath of life, like the sound of pattering rain. There they would be left to dry for use as camel fodder, the beduin knowing well the value of this diet, and it was quite usual to see camels couched expectantly round a beduin who fed them dried fish, a curious sight remarked on by Marco Polo when he passed this way.

The governor summoned a broker to discuss the arrangements for our journey to Tarim, who, like any travel agent, found the transport, negotiated the cost, and of course took his commission. We were to start off by car as there was a motorable track across the coastal plain which went for some distance into the hills, then it would be necessary to take donkeys up the long, steep pass to the plateau where cars from Tarim were to meet us. That there were already the beginnings of a motor road on this eastern route from Wadi Hadhramaut to the coast was due to the efforts of one man – Seiyid Bubakr Al Kaf.

The Al Kaf family was among the richest in the Hadhramaut; they owned great houses, had private swimming pools, imported motor cars which came by sea to Mukalla there to be dismantled and carried by camels to Wadi Hadhramaut where mechanics put them together again. They were millionaires, their fortune built by the perspicacity of Seiyid Bubakr's father, Seiyid Sheikh, who had invested money in property in Singapore and founded a financial empire. When Seiyid Sheikh died his three sons, Abdul Rahman, Bubakr, and Umar had settled in the Hadhramaut leaving relatives to manage thriving business in the East Indies. Of the three brothers only Seiyid Bubakr was a true philanthropist, spending his money freely on the welfare of others. He was determined to build a motor road from Wadi Hadhramaut to the coast and had already spent enormous sums on the workers and on bribing the tribes to refrain from damaging the road as it was built. Yet it was still nowhere near finished because of the difficulties of both terrain and tribesmen.

Having driven to the roadhead from Shihr we mounted our donkeys and, accompanied by half a dozen tribesmen, climbed the track that wound its way among the barren hills towards the plateau. The sun was setting, turning the hills a deep purple, as we reached the top of the pass after some two hours climbing, and since there was no sign of the cars we settled down for a cold night in a broken-down stone-walled enclosure intended to shelter goats. Next morning there was still no car, but we said goodbye to the donkeys and their owners and prepared to wait in the sun with the rest of the tribesmen, sparingly using such food and water as we had with us. Three beduin of the same tribe as our escort brought news that one of their number had killed a man from another tribe, so, expecting retaliation, we all set-to building up the stone wall of the enclosure. Night came and neither cars nor enraged tribesmen appeared. Harold sent off one of the beduin with a message to Tarim before we lay down for a second night on the stones, disturbed this time by one or other of the tribesmen chanting monotonously to keep himself awake and on the look out for intruders.

Two cars arrived early the following morning with Hasan Shaibi, a stalwart Saudi Arabian employed by Seiyid Abdul

Rahman Al Kaf as major domo – secretary, and we were soon speeding over miles and miles of stony wasteland, cut by deep ravines round which we had to make long detours. We stopped to lunch near a water hole and, in the surprising way of beduin, a woman with a small boy appeared from nowhere to fill their goatskins, three donkeys ambled up for a drink, and a man came to stand and stare. He was afraid we were going to take his photograph for he called out 'Last time a stranger came this way he took a photograph of my son and ever since the boy has been ill.' We often met this fear that the camera could take away something of the person photographed, and to avoid difficulties I looked through my viewfinder sideways so that I appeared to be taking what was in front of me when in fact I was snapping the person alongside.

The *jol* was not all on one level and frequently we had to cross shallow depressions where thorny trees struggled for survival. In one of these dips there was a group of about ten monkeys which hurriedly scrambled up the hillside when they heard the cars approaching. We also saw goats feeding among the branches of the trees, watched over by a woman who flapped her head cloth at them agitatedly to make them come down so that she might protect them from the dangerous motor cars. I wondered how the goats got up into the trees and found out later that the women lifted them up on to the higher branches so that they might enjoy a good meal.

In the afternoon we had to stop as large stones had been placed across the track. Four beduin came forward to ask if we had a protector from their tribe, the Ma'ara, and when they saw a fellow tribesman armed with a gun sitting in the front of our car they let us go on. Our next halt was for petrol. We came to a village where a number of tribesmen were squatting round a heap of petrol tins, brought there by camels from Wadi Hadhramaut. While the cars were being filled we were surrounded by interested onlookers, one of whom asked for medicine as she had a tummy ache and when I gave her some Epsom salts soon men, women and children were stretching out their hands for medicine. I poured the salts into as many palms as possible and as we drove away I contemplated with some misgiving what the village was going to be like next morning.

Not long afterwards we were stopped by several Jabri tribesmen who demanded money. After a lengthy argument they agreed to let us go in exchange for some rice. We drove on in the dark, having to stop a number of times as the lights of our car kept fusing. It was bitterly cold and our progress was slow because of the inadequate lights and because of engine trouble in the other car. The moon slowly rose over the horizon, a bright golden ball that helped us to see our way to bed when at last we camped exhausted on soft ground in a dip on the *jol*. We were all too tired to hear beduin blocking the track during the night but in the morning we once again found that we could not continue. This time the argument was even lengthier as they insisted on being paid a hundred Maria Theresa dollars (about £7 10s.), but finally settled for ten (15s.). These constant delays by tribesmen showed only too clearly the prevailing chaotic conditions in the country.

Three hours after giving the final protection money we reached the top of the steep pass that leads almost perpendicularly down to Wadi Hadhramaut. From there we had a magnificent view of the wide sand-coloured wadi in which the bright green patches of corn and dark green of the palm trees looked refreshingly cool, and the large white houses set in gardens gave promise of comfort and relaxation. Hasan Shaibi drew his revolver and fired several shots in the air to inform the world encircled by the high wadi walls that we had arrived at the top of the pass.

Seiyids Abdul Rahman and Umar, who lived in Tarim, were at the bottom of the pass to meet us, greeting us as old friends for we had met them both in 1934. The Al Kaf brothers were all very different. Seiyid Abdul Rahman the eldest was a dignified middle-aged man who, while anxious for peaceful development, was not inclined to take direct action himself as did his brother Bubakr, but he gave money to the Sultans who lived in Tarim and encouraged them to be more active. Seiyid Bubakr was the prime mover in getting things done, and his house in Seiyun was always filled with tribes-men whom he entertained lavishly. Seiyid Umar was half-brother to the other two, generous to foreign guests but with few interests outside his own personal pleasures, women and house-building.

The brothers lent us a house in a suburb of Tarim, which was spacious with a walled garden and a pool surrounded by a pillared terrace painted in pale green and pale blue. Ganess, our Mauritian cook, had come with us and the other servants were provided by the Al Kaf family together with a car and driver.

Chapter Three

HAREM LIFE

It was still the month of Ramadhan when we arrived in Tarim and each sunset a gun was fired, followed immediately by the voices of the muezzins ringing out loud and clear from the mosques of Tarim, said to number 360 for it was a very religious town. Boys' voices outnumbered the men's; minarets are high and it was easy for a muezzin to see women on the rooftops as he called them to prayer, therefore it was considered more prudent to use young boys who could still freely come and go in the harems.

Harold at once got down to discussions with the two minor Kathiri Sultans who looked after the affairs of Tarim under the general overlordship of the Kathiri Sultan living in the capital, Seiyun. While they discussed the future of the country Hasan Shaibi took me sightseeing and I was greeted everywhere by cries of 'Woman, Christian woman!', which brought the Tarim women, usually shy and in the background, edging forward to have a closer look. Their blue or green cloaks, the colours of which signified their position in society, covered them so completely that they were figures utterly without shape and quite anonymous. Townswomen were not expected to take any part in life outside the walls of their own homes, indeed their place in society was clearly indicated by the small mosques built for them alongside the main mosques used exclusively by men, and by the side doors which they had to use to enter their homes.

Seiyid Umar invited me to visit his Number One wife, Shfa, who was very quiet and looked worn out with child-bearing; she was then expecting her eleventh, which would be Seiyid Umar's fourteenth child as he had three more by his second wife, a younger woman whom he had married because he wanted her, whereas Shfa was a rich relative chosen for him by his father. The laws of Islam allow a man to have up to four wives *providing* he can treat each one exactly the same as the other, so that it was usually only rich men who could go in for polygamy. No Al Kaf wife would dream of sharing her home with another wife, as sometimes happened in less wealthy families, and a new house had to be built or rented each time a man married. The children of different mothers knew each other and if they were boys they would go to school together, but they tended to keep away from their stepmothers who rarely welcomed them. The fact that a number of women in the Hadhramaut put up with having co-wives did not for a moment mean that they were any less jealous or were made any less miserable than a Western woman would have been in such circumstances, but they were more fatalistic about it, saying 'It is our custom and we must bear with it'.

Seiyid Umar's small sons followed me into the harem and came forward to kiss their mother's hand and the hand of their married sister. The Al Kaf children had charming manners and the boys always looked spotless in gaily coloured sarongs, short white coats and white skull caps embroidered in gold. I found even more of these small boys in the home of the eldest brother, Seiyid Abdul Rahman Al Kaf, where I spent a great deal of time during the week we were in Tarim. It was a large, rambling house and the women's quarters were presided over by his Number One wife, Sheikha, a woman then in her thirties, attractive, with high cheek bones, large eyes, and an expressive mouth often pouted in complaint; she was bitterly critical of her husband for having another wife in Tarim and a third in Seiyun. She was also homesick for Singapore where she had been born and brought up and, although she had her mother and an aunt living with her, spoke with nostalgia of their life in Malaya where they could go about unrestricted by purdah. 'Here we are birds in a cage' Sheikha told me but though I sympathised I thought that at least she had a lovely home filled with children and with constant visitors from other houses. She rarely went out because she hated wearing the Hadhrami outdoor clothes, and even indoors refused to wear anything but the Malay sarong and *baju*,

'The harem windows looked on to the garden' (Ch. 3)

Reception room in the Al Kaf harem

Seiyid Umar Al Kaf with his daughter (in Malay dress), baby and nurse

Harold talking to tribesmen at an Al Kaf house in Tarim

scraping her hair back into a bun in Malay fashion, and
speaking Malay in preference to Arabic. One of the saddest
moments during my return to the Hadhramaut in 1963 was
revisiting this house where all the noise and bustle were but
echoes in the empty rooms, and where Sheikha, now widowed,
sat forlornly thinking still of her beloved Singapore, no longer
surrounded by her large family and numerous friends, but
fortunate in having a devoted son living with her.

After a week of conferences and social gatherings Harold
and I left Tarim for Seiyun in a car driven by fourteen-year-
old Mabruk, a slave whom Seiyid Bubakr Al Kaf had bought
for 200 Maria Theresa dollars (£15) from a beduin who had
kidnapped the boy as a baby. Seiyid Bubakr was well known
for buying slaves whom he thought were being being badly
treated, or, as in this case, had been stolen, to give them a
better home. Slaves received no wages but in Seiyid Bubakr's
household they had everything they wanted, food, lodging, a
wife, and the knowledge that they would never be sold to
anyone else.

On our way to Seiyun we stopped at the village of Hauta
for Harold to investigate the murder of a silversmith by an
Awamir tribesman who was owed four dollars by his victim.
A rather pointless murder I thought for there was then no
chance of the Awamir getting his money. While Harold went
in for a long discussion with the Sheikh of the Awamir I had
a look round and was immediately the centre of attention.
'Come to my house' whispered a dark complexioned woman
seizing my hand. 'Come to mine' said another. 'No, mine'
shouted a third. By now both my arms were being held and I
was being pulled in all directions. The strongest woman won
and, followed by a screaming crowd, we jostled each other
along the narrow lanes until we reached a small door. 'Not
here, not here' shouted several women and I was dragged
away in spite of protests by the lady of the house. Another
even more determined woman pulled me towards her front
door, where, with the help of a friend, she pushed me inside
banging the door shut behind us. The friend hastily ran
along the passage to lock another door that led to the street

c

and I was then taken upstairs, but we had not even reached
the guest room when the crowd was upon us, though how
they got in I do not know. A hefty man thrust his way through
the women, caught hold of my hand and said in English
'Come on, come on, not good here. I know, come on.' I was
annoyed at his officiousness as I had not been in the least
apprehensive among the clutching women, but as he continued pulling at me until he got me through the protesting
women and out into the street I began to wonder what he
thought was going to happen. I shall never really know but I
suspect that he was afraid they were over-excited at their first
sight of a European woman and might unintentionally harm
me: there were times later on when I was nearly stripped in
the excitement of seeing if I were the same colour all over.

When Harold had finished his discussions we continued on
to Seiyun where we had been invited to stay with Seiyid
Bubakr Al Kaf in his new house. It was a novel design for the
Hadhramaut as it was all on one floor, the flat roof parti-
tioned so that family and servants could sleep there during the
hot summer months. A wide patio surrounded a large pool,
was for the men only, while the women had lofty, airy rooms
at the back of the house, looking on to the garden. The
outside walls were painted in gay colours and inside the high
ceilings had attractive designs carved in mud which were
painted bright blue, yellow or green. It was a comfortable,
happy home in which we spent many delightful hours and
memories flooded back when in 1963 I found it in use as a
boys' secondary school with classrooms in the harem where
I had sat so often holding hands with Fatima, Seiyid Bubakr's
wife.

Fatima was a rare beauty with enormous eyes, small features, and a pale olive complexion. Though not yet forty she
was a grandmother, having been married at the age of
twelve. Her manner was serene and she was slow to anger,
but she kept a strong hand on the women of the house, both
family and servants; her personality was such that she was
consulted by women from far away, drawn to her by her
reputation for wisdom in giving advice, as well as by her

bounty, which was more sparing than her husband's because she was naturally more thrifty, but which nevertheless was always given to those in need.

The after-sunset Ramadhan breakfast had just begun when we reached Seiyid Bubakr's house and I was asked to go straight to the harem where Fatima took me by the hand and drew me down to the floor beside her, a servant brought a ewer and basin for me to wash my hands, and with a nod towards the food Fatima invited me to eat. I had scarcely met her before that evening and knew none of the family but was then introduced to Zahar, wife of Seiyid Bubakr and Fatima's second son Sheikh, who sat on my other side and looked as beautiful and elegant in her flowing Hadhrami dress as she would have done in the latest Paris fashions, for she had a grace of movement which was not characteristic of all Hadhrami women. Nevertheless the constant getting up and down from the floor, the Muslim prayers with their kneeling, rising, and prostrating, kept women supple and may have helped to prevent the stiffening of the joints which was less common among the elderly than it is in western countries.

There were several other women present whose names and relationships I failed to discover on this first meeting, but I did discover some of the complications of harem life, for while we were drinking tea after the meal we heard Saqqaf, Fatima's eldest son, call out that he wanted to come in. Zahar immediately left the room through another door and Fatima explained that a man must not see his brother's wife, nor his wife's sister, nor his wife's brother's wife, all of which made life extremely difficult when two or more married brothers lived under the same roof.

During Ramadhan night was turned into day and every evening there was feasting or visiting until the early hours of the morning. Among the visitors who came to call on Fatima were two striking-looking sisters, one of whom I soon recognized as Sherifa Alawiya, the 'learned widow' of Freya Stark's *Southern Gates of Arabia*. She shook hands all round, allowing those who were not sherifas (female seiyid) to kiss

her hand, but withdrew it swiftly from those who were sherifas and kissed her own hand instead. Then she sat down,
crossed her legs, and began to question me without waiting
for my replies, she recited verses from the Quran or from the
poets, speaking so fast that many of her pearls were lost on
me, but I gathered she was discoursing on the five senses,
saying that although Arab women did not move about freely
like the followers of the prophet Jesus, yet they saw with their
eyes, heard with their ears, felt with their fingers, and thought
with their brains, for Allah had made us all the same. Then
she abruptly asked me, 'Do you obey your husband or does
he obey you?' Before I had time to reply she continued with
a discourse on obedience. 'As a widow,' she said, 'I can do as
I like, but all these women must get permission from their
husbands if they want to go out, and if he says no then they
must stay at home.' Saadiya was but a shadow of her learned
sister, merely sitting nodding her head, although occasionally
Alawiya would turn to her for confirmation of a point or for
a word forgotten in a quotation but poor Saadiya was rarely
able to produce it. After consuming quantities of tea and
chewing raw carrots, the learned widow rose suddenly saying
she must go and was demurely followed by Saadiya. Her loud
voice had so filled the room that there seemed an unnatural
stillness when she had gone.

A day or two later Fatima and I were invited to Sherifa
Alawiya's house, a large square mansion inside a high mud-
brick wall. We drove there in a curtained car and entered by
a side door – the women's entrance – climbed two flights of
broad, whitewashed stairs to the door of the reception room
where Fatima took off her outdoor cloak and handed it to a
servant. We slipped out of our shoes and walked into the
room, shaking hands in turn with each person before sitting
on the floor beside our hostess. Like other intellectuals
Alawiya lived on spiritual rather than physical food, at least
in her own house, for there was nothing to eat but plenty of
tea to drink. The widow sat telling her beads, continually
ordering Saadiya to fetch her this book or that. I was the only
one who really listened to her, the others talked among them-

selves, but, nothing daunted, Alawiya lectured me in a voice that would have comfortably filled the Albert Hall. To my relief Saadiya, surprisingly daring, suggested we all played 'Old Man', a card game exactly the same as 'Old Maid'; but since no one was afraid of being left unmarried in the Hadhramaut it was the King of Spades, representing the dire possibility of marriage to an old man, that everyone tried to reject.

At sunset a maidservant brought round a plaited straw mat on which were newly roasted coffee beans and as we bent over it we rapturously sniffed the bouquet, with that same slow enjoyment experienced by a man with his after dinner brandy. Another servant sprinkled rosewater over our hands, the sign that it was time to say goodbye.

It did not take long for me to be completely at home in Seiyid Bubakr's house because I was so quickly made to feel a part of the family, indeed I was even allowed to meet the only daughter Sa'ud who, as an unmarried girl, was hidden in a room on the roof when strangers were about. It was thought that if these girls were seen by women other than their relatives or close friends someone might spread malicious rumours about their looks or their behaviour and thus jeopardize their chances of making a good match. Not that there would have been anything to fear in Sa'ud's case as she was extremely pretty and extremely rich, and although she was barely twelve there were already whispers of her impending marriage.

As well as the females of the family, Fatima, Salma wife of the eldest son Saqqaf, Zahar wife of Sheikh, and Sa'ud, there were always a number of other women in the house, some of whom were more or less permanent visitors, while others dropped in to stay on short visits from time to time. Among those who made it their home were 'Miriam of the Tea', stout and middle-aged, always good for a bawdy joke, and earning her nickname by presiding over the important ritual of tea-making; her niece, Ayesha, who drifted aimlessly about and spent a good deal of her time in the Sultan's harem where she had a special girl friend to compensate for an emigrant husband, and perhaps also to console her for the loss of three children who had died in infancy, a very common occurrence; there was also Raguana who, apart from Fatima, had the most outstanding personality in the harem. She was taller than most Hadhrami women, with a good figure and the striking looks of a film star, which she might well have been had she grown up in another environment for she also had a most compelling, deep voice. As the only one in the harem who could read we often listened entranced while she spoke the words of the Quran. I would watch her at the sewing-machine or coiling up her hair, fascinated by her grace and the serenity of her expression, which masked an intelligence and interest in the world around her that might have led her to a more satisfactory and fuller life had she been educated and emancipated. As it was she wasted her undoubted gifts in harem badinage and, like Ayesha, sought consolation for a husband who had gone abroad in the affection of other women.

Salma, wife of Saqqaf, was the noisiest of the household. Large and buxom with a voice raised frequently in complaint, she made quite clear her preference for her mother's house in Tarim to Fatima's house in Seiyun, but there was little she or anyone else could do about it because her marriage to Saqqaf, her first cousin, had been arranged when they were both infants and there were considerable financial advantages on both sides. Salma's mother, Sida, was sister to Seiyid Umar Al Kaf and therefore half-sister to Abdul Rahman and Bubakr, the 'half' being somewhat unusual, for Umar and Sida's mother was a Chinese woman who worked as a cook in her daughter's house. Like a number of other Chinese in the Hadhramaut she had been bought in Singapore as a child, brought to Arabia where she had become the concubine of Umar's father, Seiyid Sheikh Al Kaf, and had given birth to Umar and Sida. According to custom the children had the status of their father but their mother remained a slave. Fatima had a stepmother called Halima who was also Chinese, quite a young woman with great charm who, because she had been *married* to Fatima's father was treated rather like a governess in a Victorian household, above the servants but below the gentry. Halima, too, had been bought as a child in Singapore and I once asked her if she felt at all homesick. She replied quite simply, 'How can I be homesick for parents who sold me and for a country I scarcely know?'

She spent much of her time making the innumerable dresses worn by the family and always seemed happy, proud of her only child, Hasan, who was treated with the respect due to all young seiyids and had his hand kissed by all non-seiyids, including his own mother. He was a nice lad, unspoilt by his aristocratic position and he would often have his meals with his mother rather than join the other young men.

There was yet another Chinese in Seiyid Bubakr's house, Tiga, whose story had been much the same but she was no beauty, with a wall-eye, so she had been married off to another slave and worked in the kitchen. Slaves did not keep purdah so women and men could work alongside each other and the cooking was done by both sexes, but women did the housework in the harem and men in the men's quarters.

Conversation in the harem was quite uninhibited and I got used to being asked all sorts of intimate questions about my life with Harold, nor was there any reticence in front of the unmarried Sa'ud or any of the other children who listened to our conversations, though some of them were already married. It was quite common among the servants for the girls to marry at nine or ten, and these brides had an unnatural composure for such young children, a mixture of pride at being married women and shyness in front of their elders. I wondered whether they slept with their husbands and was assured that the marriages were nearly always consummated at once, but Raguana told me that she had been married when only eleven and had cried so much that her husband left her alone for a year or more.

Ramadhan came to an end while we were still in Seiyun, and the day before the feast that marked the end of the month of fasting, I found Fatima leaning against cushions on the floor having her hands decorated with an intricate pattern in henna that took five hours to complete. During this she directed the preparations; crockery had to be washed, the

brass polished, the coffee beans prepared, and the cone-
shaped loaves of sugar from Java cut into pieces. Carpets
were thoroughly swept to get rid of the discarded melon seeds
and date stones, the cushions shaken, and the rooms made
ready for guests.

'I need patience', Fatima said to me, 'to sit here having my
hands done when I want to be up and see to the house. If I
don't see to things myself, everything goes wrong,' a senti-
ment echoed by housewives all round the world.

Every now and then Seiyid Bubakr put his head round the
door to see how things were going. When he found us laugh-
ing hilariously over some silly joke he said to me with the air
of a father deprecating his youngsters' antics, 'Arab women
have no manners, you should tell them how to behave. They
need teaching.'

'It *is* a pity they cannot read or write', I replied.

'I don't mean that', he said, 'they need to be taught manners. If they are taught to read and write they will start
writing to men.'

Whenever Seiyid Bubakr appeared in the harem there was
an atmosphere of strain as everyone was a little afraid of him.
His voice was gruff and rather forbidding and he was very
much 'the Boss'; Fatima could not even go to bed until her
lord was ready to do so. Most of the time she bore no resentment at his authority but I did sometimes see her frown with
vexation when he refused her some request, or shrug her
shoulders with frustrated anger at his open handed generosity
which often meant more work for Fatima and more spending
of her money as well as his own.

This domination by men had the effect of making the
women more carefree, for they had few serious problems to
solve. Husbands were found for them, they did not have to go
out to work or try to compete with men in any way, and
though their lives were circumscribed they had a definite
pattern and they knew just what they could or could not do
without male sanction. None of them had the worried, anxious expressions so often seen on women's faces in more sophisticated societies; instead they were like nuns with that

composure and serenity which one associates with convent life. But being shut away from the society of men did lead at times to attachments – even passionate attachments – to other women.

The feasting after Ramadhan went on for several days during which Fatima received numerous visitors or took me out in a car with curtained windows to pay our respects to the Sultan's harem or to call at other houses. Always there was dancing – if it could be called dancing. A space about a yard square was kept clear in front of an orchestra of three women drummers where two guests at a time stood up and stamped their feet so that the bells on their anklets tinkled, or took off their head scarves, shook out their plaits and twisted their bodies from the waist until their hair was flying round them. When they tired another two took their place. Some years later I visited Knossos and this dancing was vividly recalled by the paintings of the dancing women with plaited hair, who might well have come straight from the Hadhramaut.

Chapter Four

DONKEY JOURNEY WITH SEIYIDS

Soon after arriving in the Kathiri State Harold had begun discussing with Sultans, seiyids, and tribal chiefs, the possibility of arranging a three years' truce between all the tribes, for without peace in the country there could be no orderly administration and no development. A peace conference was due to take place in Seiyun but before it opened tribesmen of the Bin Yemani tribe fired on a car that was bringing Captain Beech of the Royal Engineers to Tarim to survey the motor road. It was obvious that tribal leaders would not sign a truce unless they were assured that anyone who broke it would be punished, and so they waited with interest to see what action, if any, would be taken against the Bin Yemani by the British Government. The Kathiri Sultan, as suzerain of the Bin Yemani tribe, together with Harold, as representing the British Government, ordered the Bin Yemani to pay a fine in cash and animals by a specified date. Harold then had to go to Aden to discuss with the Resident that bombing the Bin Yemani might be necessary should they fail to pay the fine. I proposed to wait in Seiyun, but the Resident had the mistaken idea that because tribesmen had shot at Captain Beech the country was unsafe and he insisted on my returning to Aden with Harold. As this was considered an emergency, the R.A.F. were allowed to take me, otherwise women passengers were strictly forbidden, and I went with Harold to the Shibam landing strip where Flight Lieutenant Macdonald, pilot of the Vincent in which I was to fly, lent me a pair of trousers so that I could have the parachute harness strapped on in decency, but having done that, he then nonchalantly tossed the parachute into the back cockpit saying, 'You won't be needing that anyway'. I heard afterwards that it was impossible to get out of the middle cockpit, where I sat. In this age of jets and space-ships, it seems incredible that the Vincent was started by a mechanic turning the propellor. When the pilot called out 'Contact', the mechanic jumped into the back of the open cockpit and we were off. We swooped low over the territory of the Bin Yemani to give them an idea of what an aircraft could do and then swooped again over country nearer Aden where a minor war was being waged, but this time it was to drop a plum pudding on a Political Officer for his Christmas dinner. I am afraid I repaid Flight Lieutenant Macdonald's kindness in lending me his trousers by being extremely sick all over them.

We spent Christmas 1936 in Aden and shortly afterwards Harold, having finished his discussions with the Resident, was flown back to Seiyun to continue his peace negotiations with the tribes and also to try to persuade the Bin Yemani to pay their fine. As this time there was no reason for the R.A.F. to fly me, I had to follow, with our cook, Ganess, by sea to Mukalla, there to hire donkeys for the 200-mile journey to Seiyun.

At Mukalla Ganess and I were housed once again in the guest-house, and although everyone was most welcoming I felt under surveillance, particularly by Ahmed Nasir al Batati, the commander of the forces, and Seiyid Hamid, the Minister, the two leading personalities round the Sultan. The Sultan himself was very affable, even laying on a parade of soldiers and schoolboys in the palace courtyard which I watched from the seat of honour, a sofa placed at the bottom of the palace steps on which I sat sandwiched between the Sultan and his son.

I found that being without Harold more women came to see me, arriving heavily veiled at the back door, and among my most frequent visitors was Bukhita, a pretty Indo-Arab woman who invited me to visit her mistress, the widow of the Sultan's father. The Sultana was quite a bit younger than her stepson and had a small house in one corner of the compound that also enclosed the guest-house and Seiyid Hamid's house. She lived on an inadequate pension but tried to keep up the style that befitted her position. She was addicted to the betel leaf which meant that I had to chew it also as there was quite a ceremony attached to its use and it would have been impolite not to join in. Soon after we had greeted each other and had sat down on the floor, Bukhita brought a silver box and a silver spittoon which she placed in front of my hostess who, with long shapely fingers, delicately took out a leaf, pressed it open, covered the centre with a thin layer of lime, some spices and an areca nut, folded it over and over, then rose, saluted me by raising both hands to her forehead and handed it to me. I had risen also and, far less gracefully, returned the salute and took the leaf. It tasted horrible and as soon as good manners allowed I used the spittoon.

I went also to the house of Seiyid Hamid, the Minister, never imagining that this was to be our home for several years. He was without his coat or turban and with the outward signs of formality gone he was more at ease. He sat crosslegged on the floor playing with his toes in what, to judge by the double bed in one corner, was his bedroom. We talked about my journey to Seiyun as he was arranging for me to travel with two of his relations who lived in Wadi Du'an, and then presently he called his wife, Shfa, to join us. She had the long face and high cheek bones of all Du'ani women and wore the Du'ani dress of black with an orange scarf tied round her head. It was strange that throughout the Wadi Du'an every woman wore the same type of dress, black, short sleeved, gathered at the waist by a silver belt, and with a breastplate of many-coloured patches of cloth, and every single woman also wore an orange scarf. Strangest of all was their custom of wearing an ordinary finger ring of silver or gold with a stone in it through one nostril, a most unattractive adornment without any of the exotic charm of the gold stud worn by Indian women. Shfa was no exception and had a large ring jutting out of her nostril like an animal ready to be led to the market.

Seiyid Hamid was worried about his wife as she was not eating, and I think he had really invited me to give an opinion as to her condition, which we all agreed, after some discussion, was probably due to the early stages of pregnancy.

Shfa hardly said a word which did not surprise me as Arab women rarely spoke when their husbands were present.

The two relatives with whom Ganess and I set off on our journey to Seiyun were contrasting types, Seiyid Hamid bin Mustafa was tall, genial, and somewhat intellectual, while Seiyid Salim bin Bubakr was short, stout, jovial, and rather stupid. They had two beduin with them who were their cook and butler, and three others, Mautor, Ajlan and Suleiman, who were the owners of our donkeys. Mautor had been nick-named for his speed as a message carrier and he lived up to his name the morning he and Ajlan arrived to load up the donkeys. Mautor ran up and down the stairs, seizing kit-bag or suitcase, flinging them to his partner who, without more ado, tied them on to the donkeys, which in less than ten minutes were trotting out of the compound. The rest of us did not leave until the afternoon as we were to go by car for about twelve miles, as far as the motor road from Mukalla to Wadi Du'an had been completed. We were quite a procession with two cars and two small buses carrying numerous friends who came to see the seiyids on their way.

There was no sign of the donkeys at the roadhead so we all climbed on to a flat boulder to await their arrival, the men twisting their turbans round their crossed legs which apparently makes a comfortable support. As the sun set some of them got up to pray and so began a lengthy argument as to the direction of Mecca, only settled when a man from the nearby village came out with some coffee for us and was able to point the way they should face. The coffee was ginger-flavoured, a peculiar drink, common all over the Hadhramaut among those who could not afford anything better; it was made from the husks of the coffee bean which, being almost flavourless, had to be given a taste by using ginger. No water was available for ablutions before prayers and this started a discussion as to whether they were really necessary. 'Hanafis', said Seiyid Hamid with disapproval, 'do not mind if they have touched a woman between ablutions and saying their prayers, but we Shafa'is insist that we must wash again.' This made him a butt for jokes as he had touched my arm

when emphasising a point and had then said his prayers without washing. I was reminded of an old seiyid who carefully
covered his hand with his shawl before shaking mine in case
I might be menstruating. Sa'ud, when playing cards with her
brother Alawi, youngest of Seiyid Bubakr Al Kaf's three sons,
would sometimes tease him when he was about to say his
prayers by touching his hand and saying with a giggle, 'Now
you've got to wash again as I've got blood.' Men and women
after having intercourse must wash thoroughly, including
their hair; before saying prayers, and this too was a source of
ribaldry in the harem, for when anyone came in with wet
hair everyone would call out, 'We know what you've been up
to!'

We were joined on our boulder by a very ancient coal
black slave who sat on the fringe of the circle, greeted us all
and then kept up an incessant murmur of, 'Everything comes
from God, praise be to God.' This fatalism was to be found
everywhere but especially among the sick, the bereaved
and the old, and I am sure it helped them to endure their
troubles.

It was dark by the time the donkeys turned up and we
decided to spend the night in the village, indeed supper was
already being prepared for us in the house of the head man
who was quite unperturbed at having more than a dozen
people sleeping in his house. Ganess took my things to an
upstairs room where he put up my camp bed and I had an
excellent sleep broken at dawn by a strident voice calling the
faithful to prayer. We set off early along a dry river-bed green
with date palms on either bank, pursued by thousands of
flies which we could not get rid of until we reached the colder
climate of the plateaux. The seiyids were in no hurry and did
not relish long hours on the back of a donkey so we halted for
lunch while it was still quite early, and their beduin spread
out carpets on the sandy river bed in the shade of a large rock,
and placed cushions for our backs. I realized then that
Hadhramis had a better idea about travel comfort than clut-
tered-up safari-minded Europeans, for it was all so simple and
yet so adequate. Seiyid Salim inhaled long puffs from the

hubble-bubble while Seiyid Hamid read aloud an ode to a
railway train from a book of poems, and so the time passed
pleasantly until our lunch of rice and dried shark was ready.
This was followed by green tea, and then, refreshed, we were
ready for the climb up the coastal hills to the plateau, helped
on the way by Suleiman playing a plaintive melody on his
reed pipe.

Each night of our journey we slept in one of the stone shelters to be found scattered over the plateaux. They had been
built by philanthropic men for the use of travellers, though
unfortunately they were never looked after and were used as
often for animals as for humans, but our beduin spread the
carpets over the dung-covered floors and we forgot what lay
beneath. I usually slept outside, preferring the snorts of the
donkeys to the snores of the men, also there were no windows
in the shelters and, much to the seiyids' astonishment, I
needed fresh air in order to sleep, though when we had
climbed to 6000 feet it was too cold to be out of doors and I
then placed my camp bed as near to the open doorway as
possible. Going to bed was a simple process for everyone but
me. The seiyids did not wash again after their ablutions for
evening prayers, nor did they change their clothes, they just
took off their belts, wrapped their heads in their turbans, and
curled up under the blankets, saying in a whisper, 'In the
name of God' as they turned over to sleep.

In the morning Seiyid Hamid was one of the first to rise,
going outside for a minor ablution. Then, spreading out his
prayer mat in the shelter, he would turn towards Mecca and
begin his prayers, undisturbed by Ganess making tea on the
primus or by me combing my hair on my camp bed. His
prayers were like the groans of a sick man with barely a
word distinguishable; now and again he would break off to
give an order to one of the beduin. When he had finished he
got back into bed and Salim would take his place.

I enjoyed travelling in the company of these two as I felt I
was sharing in the life of the country, a part of it rather than
a stranger in a strange land. Of course on this occasion I was
travelling first class with aristocrats, with servants to wait on

us, but later I often travelled third class without servants and sharing food from the beduin's saucepan.

I was never completely happy riding a donkey because I was much too heavy for it and my long legs dangled on each side almost touching the ground. Hadhrami donkeys are extremely small but they are sturdy and surefooted on the stony mountain paths, more so than camels with their large soft pads which are better suited to the sand. There were few riding camels in the Hadhramaut, they were nearly all the heavy, slow moving baggage camels, excellent for carrying goods but not popular for riding, and for this reason the donkey was the more aristocratic means of transport. Nevertheless, I liked riding a camel, its slow progress enabling one to savour every twist and turn of the track, every unusual shaped boulder, each tiny wayside plant, and the distant views to the horizon. It was quite simple to slide down the side of a walking camel if the movement became irksome but not so easy to climb back again, and I never mastered the scramble up the animal's neck which the beduin did with the greatest ease.

On this journey the seiyids and I walked a good deal of the way which must have been a great relief to our donkeys. My little beast, Marzuk, had an independent mind and insisted on leading the caravan but then he could never make up his mind which of two tracks to follow, swerving from one to the other, so that if my thoughts were far away I not infrequently went over his head. Beduin can make or mar one's enjoyment of journeys and fortunately it was rare to find one who was disagreable, but I did not take kindly to Mautor who was bossy; he continually asked what *bakshish* he might expect, and was extremely inquisitive about my personal habits and my life with Harold. Among other things he was interested to know whether I would kiss Harold's hand when we met, as beduin wives kissed their husbands' hands, or whether we would kiss on the mouth as he understood Europeans did. He used the Arabic word for 'smell' because kissing as we know it was not customary, affection being shown by sniffing at each other's hands or cheeks. When travelling with beduin it was

Girls dressed in their best on a feast day

Hadhrami dress, worn by the author as women in purdah could not be photo-graphed

'We all climbed on to a boulder, the men twisting their turbans round their crossed legs.' (Ch. 4)

'We slept in one of the stone shelters to be found scattered over the plateaux' (Ch. 4)

to be expected that they would be curious about my habits and customs, but in general they could not have been more delightful, entertaining and attentive companions. Looking back I suppose it was strange that I never felt the slightest twinge of fear when alone with them, although I would have hesitated before walking down a lonely English lane, for I knew they would never assault a woman, nor of course do they get drunk, and I would happily have crossed any desert in their company.

Towards the end of our six days' journey across the plateaux we met Seiyid Salim's young brother with friends on their way to Mombasa, and they spent the night with us in our shelter. There was much news to exchange and they all talked at once with that eager delight we all show when seeing friends after a long absence. In the morning they parted company, first standing in a circle with hands raised saying a short prayer, then with the words, 'In the peace of God', they went their way to the coast and we went on towards Wadi Du'an without a backward glance.

The plateau ended abruptly and dramatically at the perpendicular walls of Wadi Du'an, and while I sat on a rock looking down at the green valley my companions put me to shame by changing into clean clothes, then as we scrambled down the steep, narrow track it became hotter and hotter as we left the cool air of the plateau for the stifling, dust-laden atmosphere of Wadi Du'an. The two seiyids went off to their village across the valley while I was taken once again to the fortress of the co-governors of Du'an province, the brothers Ahmed and Muhammad Ba Surra, who had been so hospitable on our first visit in 1934. They greeted me warmly and showed me to a room at the top of the house with its own bathroom where I could relax, refresh myself by ladling cold water over my body from a large earthenware jar, and put on clean clothes. I was not left long alone as the women were curious to have a look at their guest and both family and friends from neighbouring houses soon packed into the room. I was writing my diary at the time and they told me not to stop, for happily Freya Stark had been there since our first visit and had begun a tradition that all foreign women write continuously.

I stayed two days with the Ba Surras, most of the time encircled by women with whom I also went visiting other houses in different villages, crossing and recrossing the narrow valley through groves of date palms, along sandy paths built high above the cultivation, stirring up thick clouds of dust, which, together with the heat, made walking almost intolerable. My hostesses were determined to show off their guest and I felt sympathy for the bear that I remembered seeing as a child being led around as a curiosity.

The villages were all much the same, with tall brown mud-brick houses scarcely distinguishable from the brown cliffs behind them. At each house we had to climb flight after flight of twisting stairs to the women's quarters at the top. The size of the rooms was conditioned by the length of the beams available locally so that none was more than about twelve feet square with two or more carved wooden pillars supporting the rafters. There were poles fixed between the pillars and the walls for curtains to be hung so that the room could be divided when necessary, and it was not uncommon for the man of the house and his family to sit talking with me on one side of a curtain whilst neighbours sat hidden on the other side. There were no panes of glass and the open windows were shuttered by attractively carved wooden shutters; the heavy wood doors and the cupboards were also intricately carved. All doors were kept constantly locked and the women, like chatelaines of old, always carried their keys which were made of wood and shaped like outsize toothbrushes.

In every house we had to sit down on the carpeted floor, leaning against hard cushions covered with bright materials, and drink milkless tea served in glasses, and eat halwa, biscuits, tinned fruit, or the Du'an honey which is so popular all over the Hadhramaut that wherever a Hadhrami goes he arranges for honeycombs to be sent to him, packed for export in round tins made out of kerosene cans by local tinsmiths. The honey has a strong taste and is considered to be an aphrodisiac, particularly if eaten with meat, something that only men may do, as it is thought inadvisable to excite women too much.

It was a never-failing source of interest to the women whether or not I was the same colour all over. They thought I must have acquired my complexion, and the colour of my hair, from the soap I used and suggested, as tactfully as possible, that if I were to rub in oil I might become more attractive. In remote parts of the country, such as Wadi Du'an, it surprised them that anyone so unlike themselves could speak their language and they were apt to talk to me very slowly as if to someone mentally retarded, or to shout, suffering from the misconception common to English people, that if you shout loud enough at a foreigner he will understand what you say. There were often differences in local dialect which confused me and various taboos that I had to learn; for instance, in Wadi Du'an no woman mentioned her husband but called him 'he', like the Irish 'himself', but in the town of Sif he was known as 'father', and in other places just as 'man'.

On leaving the Ba Surra's home Ganess and I walked the mile or so to the village of Quweira, followed by a donkey with our luggage. Quweira was the home of Seiyid Hamid and we were to stay a night with his father Seiyid Mustafa, head of the extensive Mihdhar family. He was held in great respect so it was fortunate for me that his name was called out when he came into the room as otherwise I would have taken him for a poor hanger-on. His clothes were dirty and his manners rough, but he was friendly and thought the idea of meeting a foreign woman a huge joke. He expressed approval of my dress as it had long sleeves, since he had been shocked by pictures of European women in sleeveless dresses and short skirts, but he wanted to know why I did not wear a hat, and, as he had never before seen anyone with fair hair, why my hair was so 'white' when I was not so very old. Question after question was rained at me, not only on my appearance but on western customs generally, and even on the mysteries of wireless. I added to his bewilderment by telling him about television, which had just made its first appearance, but I could see he did not believe a word I said.

That evening my room was invaded by women and I wished I was able to paint a picture of the scene. They sat crosslegged close together on the floor, each in black with an orange coloured scarf over her hair, the one lantern from the rafter lighting up brown faces and large eyes that stared at me. They were like a coven of beautiful witches awaiting the signal to start some weird rite, but the spell was broken when my hostess, a hefty matron, pushed her way between the squatting figures and sat down beside me, asking questions in a loud voice. 'Where is "he"?' 'Have you children?' 'Why do you travel?' 'Where do you come from?' 'Where are you going?' 'Do you understand Arabic?' 'Are you a Christian?' and so on and on, scarcely waiting for my answers before asking the next question. Then she felt my dress, stroked my hair, wished me happiness, and abruptly rose and left the room followed by all the others. I was left alone to sit by the carved wooden window shutter framing the view to the silent, peaceful valley, white in the moonlight as though covered by a blanket of snow.

I was lent a large white Muscat donkey for the next stage of the journey from Du'an to Shibam, but in spite of this we were a rather tatty procession for both Ganess and I badly needed a change of clothes. Sa'id, my donkey's groom, wearing a very short *futa*, a dirty holey vest and an even dirtier skull cap, walked in front armed with a gun, then Ganess and I followed on donkeys, and behind us came two soldiers in dark blue loin cloths, also carrying guns; Mautor, the only one of the beduin going on with us, looking utterly dejected with a bad headache, brought up the rear together with another donkey bearing the luggage. It was a long, dusty, hot ride to Sif as we first threaded our way among date palms or round fields of millet, then, as the valley widened and the cultivation became rarer, plodded on across a vast sandy plain. We were all glad to see the squalid little town of Sif, which every European traveller seems to have disliked. It was no cleaner than when we had been there two years before but there was the same warm greeting from my host who this time introduced me to his wife, who had been away on the pilgrimage

to Mecca when we were last in Sif. Had she been a bit cleaner
she would have been a delightful old lady. She bustled round
me with great friendliness and told me all about her five sons
and four daughters, of whom she was very proud, especially
of Salih who had travelled to East Africa and to Aden. Perhaps it was due to his travels that he tried to be unpleasantly
familiar, no doubt he had picked up some odd ideas about
European women when he was abroad.

Short sight can be an advantage in a town like Sif; when I
took off my glasses I could not see the grime on the walls or
the bugs in the bathroom, but this did not prevent me from
having an extremely itchy night and I was not sorry when
morning came and we left for Hajarein, situated like Sif on a
spur of the wadi wall but farther up the mouth of Wadi Du'an
near where it joins Wadi Hadhramaut. At this point it was
possible to motor across the sandy wadi and I was looking
forward to being met at Hajarein by a friend from Shibam,
Sa'id Laajam, with his car. However he had not arrived by
the time we reached Hajarein at midday, so one of the soldiers set off to find the governor and ask if we could rest there
for a while. A shabby little man appeared bearing his sword
of office across his shoulders and he took us through the quite
disgusting lanes to the house of one Muhammad bin Ahmed,
whom he no doubt had deputed to be our host. Muhammad
expressed great delight at seeing us and could not have been
more friendly, but his clothes were so dirty that I knew what
his house would be like. It was even worse than I had imagined and I could hardly bear to sit on the floor among the
women who flocked round me, their faces plastered with a
yellow paste made from a plant called *wars*, and with green
or red lines painted across their foreheads so that, while they
considered they had beautified themselves, to me they looked
like clowns. Their dark blue dresses decorated with cowrie
shells were coated with grease, their bare arms and legs
smeared with *wars* and so grey with grime thay they looked as
if they were suffering from some ghastly disease. I was anxious
to leave as soon as possible but first I had to eat some cold
rice, millet bread, and round grey balls which turned out to

be squashed dates covered with ash to keep insects from eating them. My hostess took one of these balls, chewed a piece
out of it with difficulty, then offered it to me.

Such dirty villages, and people, were due to scarcity
of water. If there had been no rain for some time there was
little water for washing clothes or houses as drinking or
cooking and ablutions for prayers used up most of it, but if
you are brought up in a state of dirt you never really notice
it.

Anxious to be on our way, Ganess and I decided to ride on
but it was not long before a cloud of dust heralded the coming
of the car. A few moments later it arrived and Sa'id Laajam
jumped out, his gold teeth flashing in the sun. We packed
ourselves in, saying goodbye to Mautor and our escort who
returned to Wadi Du'an. Sa'id Laajam drove at great speed,
criss-crossing the dry river bed, leaping across the larger
stones, and making sudden detours to avoid irrigation channels or fields of wheat and we soon came to Wadi Hadhramaut where we turned eastwards heading towards Shibam.
We came to a halt beside the tall houses of the Buqri family
that stand starkly out from the flat sandy wastes around
them. This family was well known for its hospitality; the men
would shoot at anyone trying to pass without coming in for a
drink or a meal. This time Sa'id was firm, refusing to do more
than pass the time of day and give a lift to a member of the
well-known 'Aidarus family of seiyids. From that moment
everything went wrong and the poor man was called a Jonah
by all of us: first we had a puncture, then dirt in the carburet-
tor, then two more punctures. Sa'id had a supply of inner
tubes which he said were Japanese, 'very cheap, four rupees
each, but like all their goods – no good'. We spent the night
with a relative of the Qu'aiti Sultan, and next day, still with
'Jonah' (who caused us to have yet another puncture) we
reached Shibam.

This town has caught the imagination of many travellers
who have called it 'the skyscraper town of the desert', and
indeed its high houses with whitewashed roofs look from far
off like Manhattan after a fall of snow, but it is a great deal

more compact as it is encircled by a high wall and 'sky-scrapers' were the result of trying to accomodate the town's growing population within its walls. As they are built of mud bricks it has been considered remarkable that the houses have stood up for so long, and possibly one answer is that they are tapered. The sun-dried clay bricks are mixed with straw and are laid three feet thick for the first storey, gradually decreasing in thickness on each storey until by the seventh there is only a breadth of nine inches. The foundations are of stone mortared with a mixture of wood and lime and they are some five feet deep. Each house is centred round a solid pillar of mud and the stairs go up round it in a spiral. The flat roofs are whitewashed to protect them from the weather, and I was told that the houses can stand for two hundred years at least providing the 'long drops' are cleaned out regularly and kept dry.

Sa'id Laajam took me to meet his family at the top of one of the tallest of the Shibam houses. I found his two sisters having their hair dressed by servants who sat on boxes beside them, one using a large toothcomb, the other a stick made of bone. They parted the hair down the middle, then across from side to side just above the forehead leaving the front pieces loose, a sign that a woman is married, then plaiting the rest of the hair into myriads of minute plaits, a style of hairdressing that takes hours to complete and consequently is undone and redone at infrequent intervals. The reason for the trouble the two sisters were going through was that Sa'id's ten year old daughter was to be given a party to celebrate her retreat into purdah. The child was sitting against the wall, propped up by cushions, while servants drew delicate patterns in henna on her hands and feet. She sat there without saying a word, occasionally shaking her head to drive away the flies that settled on her eyes and mouth. When lunch was served on the floor, the little girl remained where she was and, as she could not use her hands for fear of smudging the decoration, a servant rolled up the rice for her and popped it into her mouth. Only the previous day this child had been able to run in and out of the house as she liked but from this day she would only be able to go out enveloped in the heavy cloak and long trousers that all Hadhrami women wore, her face covered with a black cloth, and she would have to hide in an upstairs room when married women called at the house. It was also almost the last day she would wear a coloured dress for until she became a bride she must wear only black or dark blue.

After lunching with the two sisters, who paused for a while from their hairdressing in order to eat, Ganess and I went on by car to Seiyun where we at last rejoined Harold. It had taken us three weeks to cover the ground he had flown over in three hours.

Chapter Five

SHARING A CAMEL IN WADI AMD

In Seiyun I found Harold with his hands full. Apart from his
constant travels up and down Wadi Hadhramaut in the
cause of peace, he had done all he could to persuade the Bin
Yemani to pay the fine imposed on them, but the specified
day came without their doing so. The other tribes waited to
see what would happen and were relieved to find that the
British Government was prepared to bomb the settlements of
the Bin Yemani. This showed without doubt that anyone
making the roads unsafe for travellers would be punished, and
that if the tribes joined together in a truce no tribe would be
able to break it with impunity.

Bombing began on 1st February 1937 after warnings had
been given to the inhabitants to keep well away. By today's
standards the bombs were little more than pebbles. They
were aimed at those fields or mud houses which were known
to be empty, and while the bombing went on envoys and letters were sent to encourage the culprits to pay the fine, but it
was the bombing that ultimately made the tribe give in. The
morality of bombing people into submission is arguable, and
questions were asked in Parliament from time to time about
the periodic bombing raids that took place in the Aden Protectorate, but at the time the authorities considered it to be
the best method of keeping the peace because it caused the
fewest casualties, any ground action being likely to result in
numbers of killed and wounded. Yet I feel that it was all pur-
poseless as there was rarely any follow-up (except in the
Hadhramaut) to try and build a more enduring peace. I
know there would have been much resistance among the
tribes of the Western Aden Protectorate to any interference
in their internal affairs, but had more roads been built,
schools opened, and more opportunities given to Protectorate
boys to come to Aden for secondary education, a generation

might have grown up that would have helped to bridge the tremendously wide gap between the citizen of Aden and the man in the Protectorate. Aden, because it was of use to us, was treated as a colony and developed economically and socially, but the Protectorate was largely left to its own resources because it had nothing to offer in return for money spent on it.

The bombing of the Bin Yemani had the effect of bringing in many other tribes to the peace talks until finally Harold was able to arrange a three years' truce and a document to that effect was signed by some 1200 tribal leaders. He considered this to be only the beginning as peace without good administration would be useless for any long term development projects. One of the plans he had in mind was to have the future leaders of the country educated at the College for the Sons of Chiefs in Aden, a school which he had started a year or two before. To this end I was assigned to getting the consent of the Kathiri Sultan's family for two of his sons, Hussein and Majid, to go to the college. This was one reason why I frequently called on the women of the royal household who lived on the top floor of the high palace set in the heart of Seiyun. There the wives of the Sultan and his brother, their daughters, mothers and grandmothers, shared a string of rooms and were waited on by some twenty female servants. All joined in argument with me; not one of them liked the idea of the precious boys going out of their sight: it was not customary, it was not necessary, Hussein was to be married to his cousin, a girl already sixteen which was verging on old age for a bride, and Majid was delicate, needing special food and attention. I spent hours drinking tea, chewing melon seeds, and arguing, breaking off only when they rose to say their prayers, covering themselves from head to foot in orange cloaks, standing in line murmuring, bowing to the ground, kneeling and rising, like a row of brilliantly coloured flowers swaying in the wind. I am glad to say that they finally gave in, whether because they got tired of my pestering them or because the Sultan used his authority I do not know, but the two boys went off to Aden and although their time was short at the college I hope it helped to make Hussein a better Sultan when he succeeded, and Majid a good deputy Sultan, but both of them were swept aside when independence came to South Arabia in 1967.

My next assignment was to travel from Seiyun to Wadi Amd to visit the Ja'ada tribe who were showing reluctance in signing the peace document. Numerous sections made up this tribe and they were all feuding with each other, shooting from their houses at anyone trying to cultivate his fields and generally making life intolerable for themselves and everyone else. It was then the month of Al Hajj, the month of pilgrimage which is held sacred and during which all feuds cease, so it was a good moment to penetrate the wadi and meet the people. To help me to convince the Ja'adis that peace was better than war I was to travel with Seiyid Alawi al Attas whose family lived in Hureidha, the principal town in Wadi Amd, and, being a seiyid, he was not involved in the feuds but was expected to arbitrate between the warring sections.

Seiyid Alawi's father, Bubakr, was with us when I drove the car out of Seiyun gateway on to the rough track that wound round the cultivated plots of land, over irrigation channels, and through occasional villages, to the town of Shibam, some eight miles away. There we paused for the two men to pick up clothes from a tailor. They assured me they would only be fifteen minutes: I waited for an hour and a half, becoming hotter and hotter as the crowds pressed round the car, so I was not in the best of humour when they finally returned and I made them suffer by driving at speed down the wide steps that lead from Shibam gateway to the wadi, then careering across the rough, sandy track until we reached the houses of our old friends the Buqris. Here Alawi said we would spend ten minutes, but by now my temper was restored and I was quite prepared for the expected acceptance of an invitation to lunch. After the meal there was more waiting while Seiyid Bubakr al Attas went to another room to say his prayers, but Alawi, instead of doing the same, took the opportunity of smoking a cigarette; no matter how old you are it is disrespectful to smoke in front of your father. Our kind hosts were delighted with the three years' truce, urging me to ask Harold to come and live there and make their countryside prosper again: 'We want to see our date palms and our '*elb* trees growing once more'. Pouring kerosene on to the roots of trees belonging to someone with whom you are at feud was a popular way of showing your dislike for him.

Hureidha lies on the corner of Wadi Amd and Wadi Hadhramaut and we could see its white minarets from a long way off as we drove towards it by a devious route, avoiding sand dunes, crossing stony, dry water courses, and circling the fields of wheat or millet which were guarded by mud forts from which the owners could shoot at anyone approaching. I remember one such fort that had a figure standing on the rooftop with a gun apparently ready to be fired, and finding on coming closer that it was only a propped-up dummy.

We reached the al Attas family home in the late afternoon and Alawi's many brothers and nephews were on the doorstep to greet us and to kiss the hand of Seiyid Bubakr, the head of the family. The house was unpretentious, with numerous small rooms, but the family was quite prosperous, with business interests in Java. The fact that so many of the male members had been in the East Indies added to their enthusiasm for peace and good government in their homeland. Alawi was one of several brothers and like them he had received an inadequate education which was sufficient to convince him that he should become a high government official or a successful businessman without giving him a firm grounding to succeed in anything. He was a most willing, cheerful man who subsequently took up various posts in government in Mukalla but was always seeking the rainbow of success that eluded him. He was not particularly fortunate in his matrimonial ventures either, for he had a wife in Wadi Amd and took another when he went to Mukalla, thus becoming the unhappy victim of two angry mothers-in-law, each one vowing that her daughter should not go on living with him unless he got rid of the other. If anything should be a deterrent to polygamy it is surely the thought of a multiplicity of mothers-in-law.

Shfa, wife of Seiyid Bubakr and stepmother to Alawi, was only eighteen and looked sad, unhappy I supposed at being married to a man so much older than herself. The King of Spades had certainly fallen to her. The life and soul of the harem was Jemila, a family retainer of about thirty who had adopted all the household as her own and bossed everyone in it. She was tall and sturdy but greeted us by saying, 'I thought I was dead this morning I had such agonizing pains in my stomach, but praise be to God I am all right now.' 'That's a good thing,' said Alawi unsympathetically, 'because you're coming with us tomorrow up the wadi to look after Duri.'

The most attractive members of the household were the small boys, neat and clean in white vests, long coloured sarongs, and skull caps. Their bright eyes followed my every movement and their intelligent curiosity made them ask me questions about all my possessions. They were particularly fascinated by my shoes, but rather disappointed, for Freya Stark, one of them told me, 'had much higher heels. In the name of God most high and the religion He glorifies, you couldn't walk in them they were so high'. They went to the local Quran school where, in addition to reading the Quran from beginning to end, they learned a little Arab history, grammar, and simple arithmetic, but there were no secondary schools for them to go to except a religious academy in Tarim which concentrated its teaching on early Muslim writings, traditions, and explanations of the Quran. Unless, therefore, they were sent off to the intermediate school in Mukalla or to a secondary school in Aden or the East Indies, they would just become 'lounge lizards', like most young seiyids in the Hadhramaut, sitting on the floor, drinking tea, discussing politics without knowledge or poetry, or women, wasting their natural intelligence without being aware of it, quite satisfied with their way of life.

After supper that evening my bedroom was crowded with women from neighbouring houses, dressed in bright colours but with red predominating as it was the fashionable colour for the evening. Jemila served tea and I was soon being asked all the usual questions, which by now had become very tedious. They stroked my hair, touched my clothes, and tried to reason out why I behaved so oddly, roaming the countryside without my husband. One woman had the answer, of course my husband had another wife to look after the home and I was his 'travelling wife'. There was a child of about three, Ayesha, sitting crosslegged in front of me with the shrillest voice of them all. Her body was deformed by a horribly distended stomach and I tried to convince her mother that a diet of rice, meat and hard bread might not be doing her much good. The child screamed the same question at me over and over again: 'Why do you come here? Is it because you like us? *Is it because you like us?*' In a corner, away from us all, was an old blind woman with the Muslim rosary in her hands, and as she touched each bead you could hear her murmur one of the ninety-nine names of God. She asked me to come near as she wanted to feel my face, then told me to spit on her fingers that she might rub the spittle on her eyes, but alas, I knew there would be no miracle and said that such medicine was no good. 'Praise be to God', she sighed, holding my hands in hers as if to draw comfort from them.

Many a time I was humbled by the belief in my powers of healing and wished that at least I had had some medical training. However there was one occasion, on another visit to Hureidha, when it was I who was thought to be in need of help. A crowd of Sherifas dressed in their white outdoor cloaks and looking like a posse of Klu Klux Klan were encircling me as we sat drinking coffee. One of them asked if I had any children of my own flesh and blood and when I said no, she took my coffee cup, spat in it, and handed it back saying 'I am a Sherifa, if you drink this you will have a child'. There was no escape, I had to drink it.

The morning we were to start our ride up Wadi Amd Jemila woke me early with a loud thump on the door. 'Peace be on you,' she called out, 'it is morning, drink and eat for we must be on our way.' Alawi joined me for a breakfast of hard boiled eggs, fried eggs and fried tomatoes and onions, which were not easy to eat with one's fingers, wheat bread, and sweet cakes that we dipped into honey. Then we set off, Jemila and I sharing a large bull camel. I was on the saddle over the hump and Jemila, in a black cloak and with a black cloth wound round the lower part of her face, clung on behind, her arms round my waist. She had a splendid repertoire of stirring songs to spur our beast into a canter, the only time when it was really comfortable, for a camel's trot is undiluted hell, its walking pace like a ship slowly heaving in a rough sea, but its canter is as smooth as a ride in a Rolls Royce. Unlike a horse there are no rules about riding a camel. You may have a saddle or just sit on your bedding on the hump, and you have to learn to adjust your balance as the camel changes its pace. There are no reins, only a piece of rope through one nostril which you hold in your hand and tweak if you want the camel to turn left or right. You urge it on faster with loud cries and slow it up with the Arabic equivalent of 'wo-back'. We were quite an impressive procession. Jemila and myself on the bull camel, Alawi, armed quite unnecessarily with a revolver, on a female camel with his Javanese-Arab servant holding on behind, the two beduin who owned the camels walking beside us, and a small boy who rode on top of the luggage on a third camel.

Wadi Amd is full of villages so there were many opportunities to talk about the peace. Alawi, being a seiyid, was greeted in a friendly way whenever we stopped and he would introduce me as, 'wife of Ingrams the Friend of the Hadhramaut', and tell them that I had come to talk about the truce. At the village where we lunched the first day our host showed us bullet holes in the walls. 'It is very bad,' he said, 'this killing of Muslim by Muslim. Give us peace and punish those who break it.' This was a constantly recurring theme and my answer was to urge them to sign the truce. At one place a man was at war with all his neighbours and had to keep a perpetual look-out from his fort-like home while he sent his wife out to the fields. She was not likely to be killed as it was not sporting to shoot a woman.

Our host on the first night in the wadi was a young man of

thirty-two who had had four wives and eighteen children, most of whom had died in infancy, but at the time I met him he only had two wives on the strength, who shared their husband in apparent harmony. Whe had a good supper of chicken, boiled meat and rice, which was not spoiled, as so often happened, by too much ghee. I felt distinctly queasy, however, when my host handed me a most disgusting looking object from the plate of meat. 'You must eat it,' said Alawi, 'it is the heart and is always given to important guests.' It is an organ I dislike to eat at any time but even more so when it has sinister looking strings attached, which I supposed were arteries.

Wadi Amd was very wide at its mouth where it joined Wadi Hadhramaut but gradually narrowed to its source, some 30 miles south-west, where ravines from the plateau carried down the flood waters that over the centuries had carved out the wadi. After rain it must have been a green and pleasant valley, which was no doubt why there were so many villages, but at the time we rode up it the fields were parched and the earth baked hard by the sun. We scarcely had left one village before sighting the next, each one similar to the other, with high, narrow houses built of mud bricks standing out like sand castles from the flat sand-coloured earth around them. The houses showed the insecurity of Wadi Amd, the living quarters being high above the ground and the ground floor used for animals or for storing fodder. The windows were but slits in the walls and there were high parapets round the flat rooftops. Inside they were none too clean and poorly furnished with locally made mats. The women were but a stage away from the beduin or nomadic tribeswomen, being more independent and freer than those in towns like Shibam or Seiyun. They would come into the room where Alawi and I might be talking to the men, their faces covered, and sit well back from our circle, sometimes joining in the conversation, but they only really enjoyed themselves and relaxed when there were no men in the room. It was a relief to find that the women of Wadi Amd had pleasant, quiet voices, for so many women, particularly in Wadi Du'an, spoke raucously. Their idea of beautifying themselves was to paint green lines across

The perpendicular walls of the Wadi Du'an

'Tall brown mud-brick houses scarcely distinguishable from the cliffs behind them.' (Ch. 4)

Conversation in a village street

their foreheads, down their noses, and sometimes blobs of green on their cheeks, and most of them had patterns painted in indigo on their chins. They decorated their indigo-dyed dresses with coloured patches sewn down the sides or on the sleeves and then adorned the patches with small cowrie shells or shining sequins, and nearly all of them had a coquettish patch, cut in the shape of a star, sewn on to the skirt just where they sat down.

For five days we travelled in the wadi, propagating peace, halting at every village. After greeting the head man, we talked to the crowd that quickly gathered round, and over and over again we had to refuse the pressing invitations to come inside and sit down. 'It is very difficult', said Alawi, 'but if we step inside we will have to remain for a meal and it will take us ten days to do this tour.'

Alawi never tired of telling 'these very bad people' as he called them what the Great British Government does to those who interfere with travellers or kill each other. 'But we want peace,' was what one and all said, 'we're sick of fighting. A man works in his field and is shot dead, what is the use of that? Give us peace and punish those who break it, like the Bin Yemani were punished.' The men were walking about freely as it was the sacred month of the pilgrimage, but, as one of them told me, 'If it wasn't the sacred month I couldn't walk with you like this, for we would all be in hiding, afraid to come out in the open,' and he pointed to the trenches that led from the houses to the fields, a sight that was common up and down Wadi Amd.

Each night we stayed in a village and I slept in a top room by myself, a fact which astonished the women who never slept alone in case a jinn came in the night to lure them away. Jemila prepared my bed by laying a quilt and some rugs on the floor, and she would massage my legs while telling me stories of her life, her long skinny arms whirling about like windmills and her bony fingers clutching me to emphasize a point. Then, after filling an earthenware bowl with water in case I needed a drink in the night, she would leave me to write my diary by the light of a lantern. In the morning I

E

would be woken by her thump on the door and she would
bring in breakfast, which Alawi came to eat with me, usually
consisting of fried eggs, excellent buttermilk, wheat bread and
fresh butter made from goats' milk.

When we were in the heart of the wadi I noticed that the
crowds grew bigger and bigger, which Alawi said was because
they had never seen a European before, 'and then,' he added,
'they are even more astonished when they hear that you are a
woman, which most of them refuse to believe.' In spite of his
apparent sophistication Alawi was not above being impressed
by the unknown himself; at one village where the inhabitants
were credited with possessing the Evil Eye he was careful to
dismount and walk in case the power of evil made him fall
off his camel.

During our journey Jemila and I had some trouble con-
trolling our bull camel who took a fancy to Alawi's female
and bit a large slice out of her, after which he was muzzled.
This, however, was not the only time he had misbehaved for
one morning I was called to the window to watch him 'marrying', as it was delicately phrased. The beduin did their utmost
to stop consummation, but no amount of pulling could get
the great hulking bull off the female he desired.

About half way up the wadi we met a scruffy little man
with a twinkle in his eye who had been most helpful to Van
der Meulen and Von Wissmann when they had travelled in
the Hadhramaut a few years previously, a journey recorded
in their book *Hadhramaut: Some of its Mysteries Unveiled*. They
called him Seiyid Ali the Bedui as although a seiyid he looked
as unkempt as any beduin. He greeted us with, 'Long live the
British Government,' jumped on the back of Alawi's camel
and rode on with us. We paused for a moment outside his
house to have a drink of water, and without going in or both-
ering to tell anyone he announced his intention of riding on
with us. Such minor details as a toothbrush or nightclothes
do not of course matter, it is not necessary to change your
clothes at night and a toothbrush could be cut fresh every day
from one of the *rak* bushes. His son, whom he had called
Baldwin, 'because I want him to study and become clever like

your Baldwin', waved us off, and from then on we had a useful addition to the party for Seiyid Ali knew a great deal
about the people of Wadi Amd. He was suffering from a
badly cut hand, stabbed when he had tried to wrest a dagger
from a man, and I bathed it each night with permanganate,
but Ali took his own precautions also, blocking up his nostrils
with a piece of cloth when in a strange house in case a smell
affected his wound.

At the furthermost village in the wadi we stayed the night
with a man who had been in Java, unlike most of the Ja'ada
tribesmen who tended to emigrate to Hyderabad. He had
married there and had brought back his wife and daughter
and they rather pathetically tried to bring a little of Java into
their squalid home, brightening it up with coloured carpets
and cushions, a cotton curtain over the doorway, even a pair
of shoes hung on the wall to remind them of happier days.
'In Java,' they told me, 'we walk about everywhere but here
we never go outside the door except to visit a neighbour.'
Also in this village was the tomb of the Attas family ancestor
and Alawi took me inside, pausing to say a prayer, and asking
me not to tell the seiyids in Seiyun or Tarim that I had been
inside with him as they would not approve. I had heard protests when I was taking a photograph of the tomb, but the
protestor was quickly silenced by his comrade who said, 'Don't
worry, it won't come out.'

At one village on our way back to Hureidha we arrived in
time to attend a wedding ceremony at the bridegroom's
house. Entering a walled compound where a number of men
sat crosslegged with their turbans tied round their knees, we
shook hands with each one then sat down to wait for the
bridegroom to appear. As he came out of the house surrounded by a small group of friends he was heralded by a man
beating a drum and a few shrill cries from unseen women. He
was young and goodlooking, dark skinned, and smartly
dressed in a white shirt and futa. As soon as he had sat down
a boy placed a round mat in front of him on which several of
the guests threw handfuls of coffee beans. 'Not everyone does
this,' explained Alawi, 'only those who have been invited to

lunch tomorrow and the beans will be used for their coffee.'
The same boy who had brought the mat now came out with
a tin tray and a stick, exchanged a few ribald comments with
the guests, and then pretended to attack the bridegroom with
the stick, who pulled out his dagger to ward off the boy. The
tray was then set down in front of the bridegroom and as his
father threw money on it he acknowledged the gift by striking
the tray with his dagger. Guests handed money, usually a
Maria Theresa dollar (1/6d), to the boy who called out the
names of the donors and the young man struck the tray in
thanks. This part of the ceremony ended when the boy passed
round a bowl of liquid henna into which we dipped our fingers and rubbed the henna over our hands. Then we sat
quietly talking until suddenly the bridegroom sprang to his
feet and made for the doorway as though to run away. Several young men immediately surrounded him, shouting and
barring his way, and he was forcibly led back to his place, a
part of the ceremony which Alawi could not explain. In the
usual way dancing would have followed but this was can-
celled because the family was in mourning and instead we had
some light entertainment. First Seiyid Ali the Bedui sang a
warlike song, then the local comic acted a gag farce, pretend-
ing to be a beduin from the mountains arguing about his
goats with two men picked from the audience, but the real
humour of the sketch was the way the men, who were little
more than beduin themselves, were making fun of 'ignorant
bedu'. The last item was an imitation of the way certain men
in Mukalla were said to recite the Quran. 'They are very bad
men,' explained Alawi, 'and they like to act as if they were
women, even decorating themselves with henna.'

We returned to the comforts of the Attas home in Hureidha
with the assurance that the Ja'ada tribe, or at least most of its
sections, would sign the peace document. The Ja'adis were
not only notorious as fighters but also as kidnappers and slave
traders, illegally selling men and women at the annual fairs
held in honour of local saints, a man fetching about £45 and
a woman £60. It was fairly common also for Ja'adis who
emigrated to Hyderabad to bring back Indian boys under

the pretext of giving them a good religious education and then selling them as slaves. This was brought home to Harold and me some years later when one of this tribe married a Hindu girl and brought her and her son to Wadi Amd where he promptly sold them to his brother in payment of a debt, and the brother then sold them to another tribesman. The poor woman, who spoke little Arabic, was in despair until one day she saw an aeroplane and felt sure that it came from somewhere where there must be a proper government. She made enquiries, heard about Harold and took her son and fled to him. Harold, who was then in Seiyun, brought them to Mukalla where she stayed with us until her family in India had been contacted when we put her on a ship, together with her son and another Indian boy who had had also been enslaved.

Chapter Six

FAMILY LIFE

A few days after returning to Seiyid Bubakr's house in Seiyun from Wadi Amd I was in bed with a fever and had to exert great firmness to avoid being branded with a hot iron on my back, or on the soles of my feet, the standard cure for any ailment. Sherifa Alawiya kindly sent me some prayers written on a piece of paper which was wrapped in green silk and tied round my arm. Fatima brought an incense bowl, placed a piece of paper with more prayers in the bowl and pushed it under the bedclothes. I sat with it under my legs for three minutes while the incense and the holy words were doing their work, and whether it was this treatment or the rest in bed I do not know but by the afternoon I was normal. One of the pleasures of Seiyid Bubakr's house was that there were comfortable beds, provided for foreign guests; the family preferred mattresses on the floor which in daytime could be rolled up and stored away.

It was now March and Fatima was spring cleaning when I joined her in the harem. The servants were sweeping cobwebs from the high ceilings with palm fronds, or, standing on chairs, dusting behind the garish pictures of the Kaaba at Mecca or the mosque at Medina. There were quite other kinds of pictures in the men's bathrooms, mostly of nude women, and as they were obviously European I suppose it was not surprising that Fatima asked me if I knew any of them. The ordinary Hadhrami bathroom was simply furnished with an earthenware jar of water and a wooden or tin scoop, but in Seiyid Bubakr's house there were some much more elaborate bathrooms with deep sunken baths in which there was room to swim. First you stood outside the bath to wash with soap, then plunged in. Nothing was more refreshing than this after a sweltering day in a heat of perhaps 110°.

Fatima had two grandchildren, the elder, daughter of
Saqqaf and Salma, had just gone into purdah at the age of
ten and spent most of her time in Tarim with her maternal
grandmother. The younger grandchild, Leila, daughter of
Sheikh and Zahar, was eight months old and so was kept
apart in a room on the roof, as babies had to be hidden from
strangers for two years to avoid the Evil Eye. Her parents,
however, wanted me to look at her inflamed eyes and she was
brought down wearing a tiny replica of an adult dress, and
instead of a nappy a cloth was laid under the child wherever
she was put down. Her Nanny was also her fostermother, in
accordance with another custom among well-to-do Hadhrami families by which a woman was always engaged to suckle
a baby. This wet nurse became a part of the child's life, constantly with him as an infant and acting as personal servant
to him in later life. Thus Sa'adulla, the dark complexioned
motherly woman who looked after Fatima's daughter Sa'ud,
had been her fostermother, and each of the Al Kaf sons had
a Nanny who still attended to him, looked after his clothes
and massaged his legs at night.

The baby Leila had flies walking all over her eyes and
mouth, and having washed out her eyes I suggested to the
parents that the nurse should constantly fan the child to keep
off the flies. Although Leila spent her days in a small room,
never going out for an airing beyond the flat roof outside her
nursery, she looked well, but parents and nurse were taking
no chances, the child had splodges of charcoal on her forehead
to keep away the Evil Eye. I often saw small boys dressed as
girls to delude the Evil Eye, it being thought that boys were
more likely to be harmed than the less-wanted sex.

One evening I came into the harem between the sunset and
evening prayers to find Zahar, still wearing her orange-
coloured prayer clothes, on her knees in front of Fatima talking in a loud voice, and beside her Salma, also in prayer
clothes, and evidently extremely angry. Zahar looked like an
infuriated Madonna, making lovely sweeping gestures with
her arms, whilst Salma, fat and ungainly, expostulated inco-
herently. Fatima, the arbitrator, sat quietly listening, now

and again breaking in with a comment, then turned to me to talk about our impending visit to Tarim as though indifferent to this display of tantrums. But in fact it was a serious matter – at least for Salma. She had discovered that her husband, Saqqaf, had been sleeping with the slave girl Gabula who was now pregnant, and she was particularly furious because Zahar had known all about it but had not told her. Next day Salma left in a huff for her mother's house in Tarim, saying she would not come back until Gabula had gone, for this was the last straw. She knew that Saqqaf had another wife whom he visited each afternoon, but that he should sleep with a servant while she was there was more than Salma could bear. My sympathies were with Salma but Fatima had no patience with her, for, she said, Saqqaf was not doing anything extraordinary and he wanted a son, which Salma had failed to give him. He was to be disappointed. Some days later I saw Gabula just after she had given birth. She was sitting bolt upright on the floor propped up with pillows, her fat little legs straight out in front. She had smudges of charcoal across her forehead and, because childbirth was a messy affair, she was wearing a filthy dress and lay on dirty blankets. There were neither doctors nor trained midwives in the country but there were always experienced old women and they called on the assistance of others to press their feet on the mother's back to try and hasten the birth. When the moment came the mother sat upright, knees raised and hands pressed hard on the floor while those around her encouraged her with cries of, 'Push, push', or 'Praise be to God, praise be to God'. Meanwhile the 'midwife', carefully avoiding looking what she was doing as that would be indecent, fumbled underneath the mother's dress to catch hold of the head.

Gabula, having endured all this, had given birth to a still-born child. 'What did you think of having a baby?' asked 'Miriam of the Tea' cheerfully. Gabula shook her head dolefully, clicking her tongue against her teeth to express disgust, but then poor Gabula had nothing to show for her pains.

There is a routine in the daily life of the harem just as there is in any other household. Fatima spent the first part of each morning ordering the meals and supervising the work of the servants. Breakfast was served to the married couples in their rooms, the single women eating in one of the small communal rooms of the harem which were used when not entertaining a large number of guests. After breakfast Miriam arranged the samovar and all the equipment for tea-making to be ready to start serving the almost non-stop tea as soon as anyone came in and sat down. Raguana and Halima might have sewing to do, sitting crosslegged on the floor in front of the sewing machines perched on low tables, turning out dresses for the household, or perhaps for Sa'ud's trousseau, but this was never mentioned except in a hushed whisper because traditionally a bride was not supposed to know that she was shortly to be married. It seemed to me that Sa'ud led the dullest life: she did no domestic work, no cooking, no sewing, but sat around all day long looking at dress materials, playing with her bracelets, or just giggling. Her one daily chore was to go to her father's bedroom to say good morning and kiss his hand, otherwise from the time she got up until she went to bed she drifted from room to room watching everyone else.

The day was broken up by the times of prayer. At noon Fatima would lead the women in saying the midday prayers, then change into a clean dress since the one she wore in the morning was often splashed with grease from the kitchen. Sometimes there were guests for lunch, but whether there were or not the meals were gargantuan, consisting of Javanese as well as Arab dishes. There is an idea that Arab women eat the remains of the meal served to the men, but in all my experience of well-to-do, moderate, and poor homes, I never saw this happen. Certainly servants often cleared the dishes after their masters or mistresses had finished, and children would sit down when their elders had risen, but men and women usually ate at the same time, although apart, and were served from the same kitchen.

There were prayers again in the mid-afternoon, a time when we drank quantities of milkless, heavily sugared tea, played cards, or just talked, then at sunset the women rose to put on their prayer clothes once again. If no visitors were expected they often wore these brightly coloured robes until the evening prayers, after which they changed into yet other dresses for the last meal.

Visitors to Fatima's home were frequent and Sherifa Alawiya was often there to give us sermons, holding her toes with one hand and waggling the forefinger of the other. The women took religion as part of their daily lives, accepting all that they were taught, and I was touched when Fatima asked me if I would pray with them and say, 'There is no God but God and Muhammad is the prophet of God,' because then I should not have to go through fire to attain paradise and we would be sure of meeting again. 'Of course I may not go to paradise either,' she added, 'as I'm very bad. When I pray I don't think what I'm saying but my thoughts go wandering off to the kitchen or to somebody's new dress.'

On this occasion our conversation was serious but most of the time in the harem we talked trivialities, and I was often struck by the contrast between the conversation of men and women. The men would discuss politics or history or poetry, which would have bored most of the women just as they were not infrequently bored by Sherifa Alawiya, yet with their intelligent minds they might so easily, with a little education, have entered more fully into the lives of the men. 'They are no better than sheep,' I have heard men say, but whose fault was that? The men were afraid that if women were taught to read and write they would want more freedom, and with freedom there would be an end to morality. Ideas about immorality were often a reflection of the men's ideas about the behaviour of women in the west who kissed in public, wore indecent clothes, and generally behaved in a manner which no Muslim would like to see his daughter imitate. Rahima Jaffer once told me that in Aden many Arabs were convinced all European women were immoral as they could not see how a woman could dance in a low evening dress with a man if she did not also sleep with him. In Hadhramaut the men seemed to think that so long as the women had no opportunity of meeting men they would lead chaste lives, and as far as men were concerned this was largely true, but when young women had their passions roused by early marriage and were then frustrated by divorce or the husband emigrating, it was not surprising that, having no outlet for even a mild flirtation with a man, they turned to their own sex.

Sa'ud's wedding, which was to take place in a few weeks time, was to be an unforgettable occasion as Seiyid Bubakr was the best known man in Hadhramaut and hundreds of invited and uninvited guests were likely to turn up. The cost would be enormous, and Fatima, though excited, was anxious about the amount of money Seiyid Bubakr was proposing to spend. She always felt he was extravagant and told me that he had sold some of her gold jewellery for over a thousand pounds to help to pay for the new house. 'All his money goes like this,' she said blowing on her outstretched hand. But he was not at all extravagant on his own account; most of the money he spent went to others. No poor man was ever turned away without food, and he was always finding ways of trying to improve the people's standard of living, by importing engines to draw water from the wells, by digging new wells, by buying machinery for agriculture, helping to build roads, contributing to schools, and continually handing out gifts to tribesmen in the cause of peace. Had he been able to look into the future perhaps Seiyid Bubakr would have been less generous, but who at that time imagined the changes that would so soon take place in Java and Singapore, changes which would halt the flow of remittances, life-blood of the Hadhramaut.

The gold ornaments worn by the women were considered to be investments and Fatima was prepared to give many of her own pieces of jewellery to Sa'ud as a wedding gift. I watched her one morning as she weighed gold bracelets, gold necklaces and gold anklets against Maria Theresa dollars, twelve of which equalled a pound weight, and then she took me to a room lined with cupboards to see the bride's trousseau. There were hundreds of dresses stacked one on top of the other, alongside high piles of bodices, petticoats and the fashionable red nightdresses – panties were unknown. Other shelves were laden with glasses, cups, teapots, bowls, jars, silver dishes, brass trays, samovars, bottles of scent, enough combs to last fifty people a lifetime, packets and packets of safety pins, anything that Fatima thought would come in handy for Sa'ud's future home.

Chapter Seven

A WEDDING AND AN ADOPTION

When we returned to Mukalla from Seiyun in the spring of 1937 there was peace in the Hadhramaut; as Seiyid Bubakr said, 'People now say, "Go in the peace of God and in the peace of Ingrams"'. Consequently when we were back in Mukalla we found a much less suspicious atmosphere; it was appreciated that Harold had achieved something no one else had been able to achieve and he was greeted by everyone as, 'Friend of the Hadhramaut'. I was made strikingly aware of this changed attitude when some children, who always reflected adult opinion, called after me, as they often did, 'Christian, Christian', but immediately a small boy cried out, 'She is not a Christian, she is the female Ingrams,' I knew we had been accepted.

The Qu'aiti Sultan gave us the house in Mukalla that had once been occupied by Seiyid Hamid the Minister who was now out of favour and had retreated to Wadi Du'an. It was a fine looking house from the front with an imposing pillared portico, but, like a piece of stage scenery, not to be looked at from the back. We were soon settled in, combining an Arab life with our own English way of living. Harold had his offices on the ground floor and on the floor above there were two reception rooms, one large, well carpeted and with cushions round the walls, the other, which was much smaller, had tables and chairs. The bedrooms led off the flat roof on which we slept during the summer. There were no lavatories, only 'long drops' with the usual holes over which to squat and our bathrooms had only earthenware jars filled with water. We installed thunderboxes as being more comfortable than squatting and rigged up a very insecure contraption as a shower.

In the early summer of 1937 we received an invitation from Seiyid Bubakr to attend the celebrations for Sa'ud's wedding. The marriage itself would be carried out privately between the respective fathers, the bridegroom and the Qadhi, but the celebrations were to last for several days. The road from Shihr to Tarim had at last been completed so we were able to go by car and after a long day's journey we reached Seiyid Bubakr's house where we found the celebrations for the bridegroom were being held. His old seven-storey house in the town was reserved for the women and as soon as I had bathed and changed into my best sarong I drove over to the brightly lit house, resounding with the beat of drums and the shrill cries of women. The courtyard was tightly packed with women sitting on mats. I took off my shoes and holding them in my hand began threading my way between the rows, treading on toes, being pushed here and there, while every now and then someone twisted me round to have a better look or seized my hand to kiss it. Sometimes I saw a face I knew and shook hands with what I hoped was the hand that belonged to the face. I found Fatima by the front door looking very lovely in a white silk Malay coat and sarong with white flowers in her hair, not at all hot or bothered, in spite of being crushed in on all sides and with drums beating in her ears.

Her daughter-in-law, Zahar, took me straight upstairs to the room where Sa'ud was having her hands and feet hennaed. All pretence was now over. It had been the duty of her Aunt Sida from Tarim to break the news of her marriage to her in the traditional way by calling her from her room, then catching hold of her and crying loudly, 'We are going to veil you and henna you, for you are to be the bride of Mashur.' Sa'ud promptly burst into tears, which was expected of her, and was half carried to another room where she was dressed in red, the first time she had worn a coloured dress since going into purdah as a child of ten. A black veil was thrown over her head and face and she was made to sit down on cushions, her legs straight out in front resting on pillows, her arms stretched out to the side also on pillows. Two women then began the long task of decorating her hands while two others painted her feet. Sa'adulla, her Nanny, sat on her left side, her Aunt Sida on her right, and with short breaks these two remained beside her all through the celebrations. A servant girl fanned her continuously, to keep her cool and to keep the flies away.

Sa'ud was more fortunate than most girls because she had been consulted about her husband-to-be. She was not told when she would be married but her father had asked her whether she liked the idea of one day marrying Mashur, a distant cousin whom she had known as a small boy. Had she not wanted to marry him, Seiyid Bubakr would not have insisted, but to Sa'ud marriage was inevitable and desirable, and so long as the bridegroom was young, one man was as good as the next.

The celebrations went on for almost a week. Every day hundreds of men and women were fed on the traditional rice and boiled mutton, while relatives and close friends had more elaborate meals in the family dining-room. It was all well organised. Friends who came from other towns brought their servants and were given rooms in which to put their clothes and to sleep, get away from the crowds or talk to their friends. Guests who lived in Seiyun brought their maids to do their hair or help them to change their clothes, which they did in any odd corner several times a day. Tea was served all day long, and there was a continuous stream of women bringing up water-skins to fill the earthenware jars in the bathrooms. Cooking was done on the ground floor or in the back court-yard, and I caught one nightmarish glimpse of four women sitting inches deep in onion skins peeling for all they were worth.

Only very intimate friends were allowed to see the bride before she had spent her first night with her husband so until then Sa'ud was kept upstairs in a locked room. I felt very privileged being allowed to sit with her the second day and watch her having her hair dressed as a married woman, with two pieces left loose on either side of the forehead. This made her giggle shyly, but Sa'ud who was only thirteen, was pleased at being so important, frequently jumping up to the window to see the crowds in the courtyard. On the third day of the celebrations she put on her wedding dress of red and the traditional coarse-haired wig with an ornamental headdress, a curious and ugly custom which no one could explain. Then, covered with gold ornaments, her arms held on either side by her aunt and her Nanny, she was escorted down the stairs to the bridal bedroom, followed by Fatima, other members of the harem, and a host of servants uttering shrill cries. I was told that once alone with the bridegroom a bride must not utter a word as he takes off her ornaments one by one, not even if he fumbles trying to undo the numerous clasps of her necklaces. Seiyid Bubakr, according to Fatima, was so bored with all this that on their wedding night he took a pair of scissors and cut the necklaces off her.

The morning after the wedding night the bridegroom is woken early and sent out of the room by the women servants who then wash the bride and allow her to sleep. I had been asked to come early in the morning as there was to be a family ceremony which I was invited to attend. Sa'ud, dressed in green and gold, sat on a mattress leaning against the two bridal pillows embroidered with gold tinsel and with propitious texts written on calico pinned to them. While she sat enthroned her father came in with the father of the bridegroom. Mashur looked sheepish in an orange silk coat with a sash of red and green and a white scarf falling from his seiyid's hat. He sat opposite Sa'ud who kept her eyes tightly closed. A servant passed round an incense bowl for us all to waft the smoke over our faces, and another servant came in with freshly roasted coffee beans on a plaited straw tray over which we bent our heads to sniff the bouquet. Then came cups of coffee. Nothing at all was said, and presently the men got up, placed money in the bride's lap, and went out.

As soon as they had gone Sa'ud's attendants put on her wig again and three women with drums came to lead the way downstairs. Behind them servants danced round and round, clapping their hands and ululating, two carried the bridal cushions on their heads, another carried a bowl of incense. Then came Fatima, looking very tired, and behind her Sa'ud, supported on the arm of her aunt and clanking with thick

View of Shibam

Wadi Amd (Ch. 5)

'The women of the royal household lived on the top floor of the Palace in the
heart of Seiyun' (Ch. 5)

Seiyid Bubakr Al Kaf at dinner with Hasan Shaibi

silver anklets loaded with bells. The rest of us, family, intimate friends, and still more servants, brought up the rear of
the procession. With a wild crescendo of drumming, ulula-
tion, and piercing cries of, 'Praise to Muhammad, praise to
the Prophet,' Sa'ud entered one of the large reception rooms
where she was lowered on to a mattress and her veil lifted so
that all the guests might see her face while Sa'ud kept her
eyes demurely lowered. This was the exposure of the bride on
the morning after the wedding night, when she was accepted
into the world of the married women. Next day she was ex-
posed in a similar way for about two minutes to the women
who thronged the courtyard. Then at last the party was over.

During that summer of the wedding Harold and I spent a
lot of time travelling between Mukalla and Seiyun, made so
much easier now that we could cover the distance by car.
Immediately after the wedding we returned to Mukalla
where Harold now had clerks from Aden to help him cope
with the office work that had increased tremendously as he
began to organise government services, with the full support
of the Qu'aiti Sultan. But he was also needed frequently in
Seiyun to advise on a tribal dispute or some other local problem. On one of the visits to Seiyun he had to settle a feud that
had arisen over a tribeswoman who had been wrongfully
enslaved as a child. He said that the woman in the case should
be freed and allowed to start a new life in another area with
the man she was going to marry, who came from a distant
part of the country. She had with her a baby daughter, Zahra,
born of a previous marriage, and she brought the little girl to
Harold to ask whether we would be prepared to adopt her.
Zahra seemed very young indeed as she did not crawl nor
utter a sound, but just sat on the floor, her large eyes fringed
with long curly lashes gazing at us with a most solemn
expression. Her adoption was arranged as officially as it
could be with both the Kathiri Sultan and Seiyid Bubakr Al
Kaf signing the piece of paper that gave us a daughter. Many
years later when I had to get a passport for Zahra, then a
schoolgirl, I was asked for her birth certificate. Anticipating
this I had taken the declaration of adoption to the Passport

F

Office and said that this was all I could produce as there was no register of births, marriages or deaths in the land where Zahra had been born. As it was all in Arabic I was asked to translate. I began, 'In the Name of God the Compassionate, the Merciful . . .' It was enough – I received the passport with no further trouble.

At first Zahra yelled every time I went near her, probably because my colouring terrified her, as she had only been used to dark faces and dark clothes. Harold, who had returned to Mukalla, sent me a fat, jet black motherly woman to help and she smothered Zahra in her comfortable bosom from which safe refuge the child would gaze at me until gradually she got used to the strange apparition that had entered her world. The three of us returned by car to Mukalla and I was delighted when, at our lunch halt by the side of a dirty rainwater pool, Zahra spoke her first word – *Ish* – which I soon learned was a demand for a drink of water. It was obvious that she was suffering from malnutrition so we sent urgent cables to friends in London for cod liver oil and Glaxo. She lived on these for some months until I had the opportunity of taking her to Aden to seek advice from a doctor. By then she could stand, toddle and attempt quite a few words and I now put her age at perhaps fifteen months, but the doctor surprised me by saying that she must be at least two years old and her development had been retarded because of rickets. The disease had affected her feet which were inclined to turn in, so we sent to London for special fitments for her shoes, and with their help, normal food and still more cod liver oil she gradually caught up with well-nourished children of her own age. The motherly Nanny was replaced by Halima, a slim, pretty Somali who, being unveiled, could take her out for walks and could mix freely with the men servants. In fact she mixed so freely that eventually she married Ganess, our Mauritian cook, and led him a tempestuous life with her violent temper until one day the marriage came to an end as abruptly as it had begun.

Chapter Eight

LIFE IN MUKALLA

In August 1937 the Qu'aiti Sultan signed an Advisory Treaty with the Government of Aden, stipulating that Harold should be his first Resident Adviser, and some months later a similar treaty was signed by the Kathiri Sultan, Harold then becoming Adviser to both states. These advisory treaties laid down that the Sultans would accept the advice of the Resident Adviser, 'in all matters except those concerning Muhammadan religion and customs.' They were a new departure in policy, hitherto the Government of Aden had maintained the principle of non-interference in the internal affairs of the states of the Protectorate, but following Harold's report on conditions in Hadhramaut and the urgent and earnest requests for help from influential leaders the Aden Government reconsidered its former policy.

In spite of being a Colonial official Harold had quite uncolonial ideas about how Hadhramaut should be developed, and he was determined that Hadhramis should run their own country and that it should never become a 'colony' in any sense of the word. He saw himself as an Adviser in its truest sense but, because he was the first to hold the post and so much had to be started from scratch, it was inevitable that he had to give a good deal of direction, but he never lost sight of his objective – that Hadhramaut should stand on its own feet. The fact that his successors adopted a more paternalistic attitude was to my mind a contributory cause of the troubles that arose in the sixties.

The work of the office increased enormously and there was plenty to do outside also, watching work on the new barracks, seeing how far new roads had progressed, visiting schools and, in my case, accepting invitations to meet the families of the men who were constant visitors to our house. For some time Harold and I had been wearing Arab clothes when we were outside our own home, a custom that began when Seiyid Bubakr gave Harold his first *futa* and Fatima asked me if I would wear a sarong, saying it would be much more comfortable than a short dress when sitting on the floor. The sarong, however, was not worn as an outdoor garment and I felt unbearably conspicuous walking through the streets in a short skirt, so I adopted what at that time was the outdoor dress of women in Syria, a long black skirt and a cape that covered head and shoulders. This was no protection against the sun but it hid my hair and the low neck line of my 'Western' cotton dress. Wearing Arab clothes can be described as 'dressing-up', but it has to be remembered that we were the only Europeans in a country where traditional customs were held very dear and where there was much suspicion of Christians. To be the only woman in a country showing her legs, or her hair, does not help to make you feel at home, whereas I found that conforming as far as one could to local customs made one not only more acceptable but more at ease. Returning to the Hadhramaut twenty years later I had no hesitation in wearing my ordinary summer clothes out of doors, but by that time Hadhramis had grown accustomed to the habits of Europeans, and it would then have been play acting to have walked about in anything but my usual clothes.

There were two ways of giving a dinner party in Mukalla, sitting stiffly on chairs using knives and forks, or cross-legged on a carpet eating with your fingers. The Sultan entertained in both ways, so did we, but only about a dozen could comfortably sit round our dining room table whereas we could – and often did – entertain sixty or seventy in Arab fashion. It was not long before experience had taught Ganess, and me, just what was needed for such a party. We counted on half a pound of rice and half a chicken (they were very small) for each person, two kids or lambs roasted whole, and a sheep which was cut up and cooked in a variety of sauces. Local fish was excellent, there was not much in the way of vegetables except onions, but there were delicious bananas and occasionally mangoes and figs. These meals were surprisingly cheap, mainly because everyone drank water, and as everyone ate with their fingers they were much less trouble than European meals since there was little to wash up, but we had to engage extra help to clean the mountains of rice and Halima brought in some of her Somali friends for this job. Our guests were men only, (I gave separate dinner parties for my women friends) and as they arrived they slipped their sandals off at the door, crossed the carpet shaking hands with each guest already there and sat down against the wall wherever they liked, but room was always made for important personalities to sit near the host. After some quiet conversation the double doors into the dining room were flung open and a servant stood at each door with a ewer and basin. As we walked through the doorway we held out our right hands over the basin for the servant to pour water over them, then we sat down anywhere we liked round the long white tablecloths spread over the floor, leaving the guest of honour to sit beside the host. All the food was laid out on dishes on the cloths and each guest had his own plate on to which he scooped whatever he fancied from the dishes near him, then he got down to the serious business of eating. There was no conversation. As soon as anyone had finished he got up, regardless of whether other people were still eating, went to a corner of the room where a servant waited with basin, soap and towels, washed his hands and face, and returned to the other room where he resumed his place against the wall. When everyone had left the dining room milkless tea was served in small glasses, and the hookah passed from mouth to mouth. Conversation then became animated but no one stayed long for Mukallawis went to bed early and by ten o'clock the last guest had gone home.

Alcohol was prohibited by law and we never had it in our house even for non-Muslim guests. There were many who thought Harold was unnecessarily rigid over this but I think it would have been wrong to have made an exception of ourselves, especially as we were the first Christians ever allowed to live in the country. At that time I am sure there was scarcely anyone who drank spirits, though I remember one occasion when a Mukalla seiyid came into my office obviously having had too much to drink, sat down and boasted, 'I drink whisky like the English.'

My work in the office consisted mainly in producing a weekly intelligence summary and dealing with confidential papers, but when Harold had to make his frequent journeys to Seiyun or to Aden a good deal of variety was added to my daily routine. I noted a day's work in my diary during the winter of 1937 when Harold was away from Mukalla:

> Breakfast at 7.45 with Zahra. Saw Muhammad Ali (Chief Clerk) to arrange despatch of petrol and oil for the R.A.F. Then Haddadi (of the Mukalla Treasury) came to see me about the letter to sub-accountants and I agreed to send a draft over to the Sultan. Also discussed repairs to the Fuwa road and customs duty on wireless sets. Promised to write H. about this. Counted money in the safe and found one rupee too much – tiresome. Acknowledged Antiquities Ordinance from Sudan Government. Two Nahdis came to complain about their pay and I said they must complain in writing. Slept after lunch then had a walk along the beach with Zahra. We built sand castles. Back to shower and change. Saw Msellem (State Treasurer) regarding petrol for government cars, also difficulties of taxation at Dis and a rise in pay for the Sanitary Inspector. Salim (clerk) still ill so sent him quinine. Did some registering of papers with Souza (another clerk) and began a clean up of Ahmed Hassan's desk (interpreter who had returned to Aden). Dinner and listen to the wireless.

A major chore in the office was the issuing of travel documents, especially to those who wanted to go to East Africa when the monsoon was blowing in the right direction for the dhows that sailed from Mukalla to Mombasa and Zanzibar. At that time of the year hundreds of tribesmen converged on the Residency and as practically none of them could write we spent hours filling up forms and taking thumb prints. If they belonged to tribes considered to be within the jurisdiction of the Qu'aiti or Kathiri Sultans they were supposed to take papers from the state governments, but it was more than one's life was worth to ask one of them if he were a subject of the Qu'aiti or Kathiri Sultan. One foolhardy clerk did this and nearly had his throat cut by the tribesman who drew out his dagger crying furiously, 'I am subject to no one.' One season there was an epidemic of some kind in Mombasa and we were asked by the Government of Kenya not to issue documents for that port, so whenever a man asked to go there I would tell him how much nicer it was in Zanzibar and persuade him to go there instead. I often wondered if the authorities in that island noticed the extra influx of Hadhramis.

While we were hard at work in the office, Zahra played upstairs, getting stronger every day and asserting her independent tribal spirit by refusing to stay in the wooden pen built for her by the local carpenter. There was a good deal of curiosity about Zahra among the women in Mukalla and when I was invited to their homes they often asked me to bring her along with me. I was never quite sure about their reactions; they would say, 'God bless you for looking after the orphan and the abandoned,' but I felt there was an underlying fear that we would turn her into a Christian.

Purdah was just as strict in Mukalla as in Wadi Hadhramaut but being a seaport with ships calling there from distant places, the women were more aware of the world outside than those living up-country. Quite a number of them had been to Aden and even to India. Their clothes and their food were influenced by the connection with Hyderabad, saris were sometimes worn and curries were popular. The typical Mukalla dress was long, high waisted and straight, quite unlike the voluminous shapeless dresses of Seiyun or Shibam.

As the Sultan's son, Awadh, lived in the same compound I was frequently in his house and found that his marital problems were like 'the continuing story of Peyton Place'. He was for ever seeking a wife who would give him a son and I was not surprised when one day the pretty, young, ineffectual Salma called me over and weeping bitterly told me that Awadh had decided to take a second wife. To make matters worse he had described the bride to be as being more beautiful than Salma. I could do little about it but talked to Awadh who again stressed that all he wanted was a son and heir. He added that there was no reason for Salma to stay if she did not want to, but a young girl felt a certain proud satisfaction in being the heir apparent's wife, a position not easy to relinquish. Consequently Salma gave in and Awadh, rather nervously, brought the two wives together. A day or two later I saw them sitting side by side trying to look as if they were enjoying it and they showed me the identical gifts of cloth and jewellery that Awadh had given them. They held a party at which they danced together to show their friendship, but fat and cheerful Fatima – the new wife – was the stronger character of the two and soon ousted Salma. Fatima then prepared to use all her wiles to keep Awadh, incessantly consulting me about ways and means of producing a son. It was not long before she, too, had problems and I was asked to come and discuss what was to be done. This time the trouble was over Zeinab, one of the slave women favoured by Awadh. It had been discovered that she had paid a holy man to write on pieces of paper 'You must love only Zeinab' and had placed them under Awadh's mattress, in his pillow, and under the carpet where he sat. Fatima's problem was how to dispose of both Zeinab and her bits of paper. We agreed there was no way to be rid of Zeinab who, being one of the Sultan's slaves, could not be discharged, but we could at least get rid of the magic words – but how? I suggested burning them. This was no good because the charred words would float about in the air still bearing their message. It was the oldest and wisest of the slaves who finally found a solution – she would carefully wash out every letter of every word then throw the papers down the 'long drop' and they would be taken away and disposed of for ever by the man who had the unenviable job of cleaning it out. Whether it was due to this or Awadh's natural tendency towards variety, nothing more was heard against Zeinab but there were several more brides before he finally achieved a son.

About every three months I went to Aden to buy supplies for the next three months, things that were not to be found in

Mukalla, such as the particular brands of tinned butter and cheese that we liked, clothes, books, or powder and lipstick. Sometimes I took Zahra with me to see the doctor and in the autumn of 1937 she and I were in Aden when Anton Besse, the enterprising millionaire Frenchman who later founded St. Antony's College, Oxford, started a regular air service to the Hadhramaut. He asked if I would like to return to Mukalla on the inaugural flight, so Zahra and I joined the pilot, co-pilot and an interpreter in the fragile, leaflike aeroplane. We took off from Aden early in the morning and after three hours we were approaching the range of hills near Mukalla when suddenly the aircraft made a violent downward swerve. We had run out of petrol in the starboard engine. It was not possible to get enough lift to clear the hills with the one remaining engine so the pilot decided to make a forced landing. Understanding nothing about the mechanics of an aeroplane I felt that at any moment we would drop like a wounded bird to the ground and only hoped the pilot would land before that happened. He circled down to have a look at a dry river bed but thought it was too rough so he turned the aeroplane towards the beach. 'Hold tight,' he called out as we came in to land. I was so relieved to be near the ground that I stopped being afraid although later I realized that it was the most dangerous moment of all. The pilot landed magnificently with no more than a bad jar and a horrible scraping sound. The machine ran on for some way but we came to rest smoothly and the only one of us quite unperturbed was Zahra, who had slept through it all.

There was no sign of life on the beach but three fishermen at sea in a boat came ashore to have a look at us. One of them agreed to take a message to Harold but told us it would take him six hours to reach Mukalla. We also asked him to let the nearest village know what had happened and to send us some water, and it was not long before the head man of the village came along on a donkey with several companions and a goatskin of water. When some fishermen brought us their catch we cooked the fish on an open fire and sat down to quite a cheerful picnic. Zahra showed her capacity for adapting herself to any circumstances and made no complaints over her diet of rusks and fish. Meanwhile Harold had been waiting for us at the landing strip and after an hour or two returned to Mukalla expecting to find that a wireless message had come in to say the flight had been delayed. Six hours almost to the second after our messenger had left us he arrived at Mukalla and his news caused quite a stir, but at least it was known that we were all safe. Harold left at once by car to the foot of the hills that we had failed to fly over and hired a donkey from the nearest village, arranging also for a boat to come round the headland and pick us all up in the morning. He had a long ride before he reached our camp in the middle of the night to find us all fast asleep under the wings of the aeroplane. In the early morning the boat appeared and we were rowed through a rough sea to the point where Harold had left the car.

In spite of this inauspicious start, the air service continued fairly regularly and the Hadhramis rather surprisingly took to the air eagerly. Surprising, because while we graduated through train and car to the aeroplane, many Hadhramis had never even seen a car before they took their first flight. This small beginning developed after several years into the daily service of Aden Airways, an offshoot of B.O.A.C. Its sophisticated connections, however, did not prevent Aden Airways from being delightfully informal. In 1963 I travelled in their aircraft a number of times and on one occasion the goat that one of the Sultans had bought in order to breed a new strain wandered from the luggage compartment into the cabin among the passengers. The steward was also the tally clerk and the ticket collector and at every stop had difficulty in preventing more passengers boarding than were entitled to do so; overloading meant nothing to them, nor did the signs 'Fasten Seat Belt' and 'No Smoking'. In any case it was almost impossible to fasten a seat belt round a woman enveloped in a voluminous black cloak holding a baby at her breast. Neither men nor women passengers showed any apprehension, but I noticed they never failed to whisper, 'In the name of God,' as we took off.

Chapter Nine

JOURNEY TO HAJR PROVINCE

The Qu'aiti State was divided into five provinces, among them the Hajr province which we had not visited. It took its name from Wadi Hajr which ran from the north into the sea, a unique wadi in the Hadhramaut as it had a river flowed along much of its length and this meant that the province held possibilities for agricultural development. One of my early assignments after we had settled into Mukalla was to make a trip into Hajr to report on the conditions that I found there. Salih Ali, the soldier who had been a good companion on our first journey in 1934, was always ready to give us a hand and he volunteered to come with me. His manners were impeccable and his bearing dignified, as befitted an 'officer and a gentleman', and he reminded me of some character in a Victorian novel. He was certainly Victorian in his attitude to women as whenever he left Mukalla he locked his wife into the house so that she could neither go out nor receive visitors. He assured me that this was done for her peace of mind but, like the Crusaders, I think he preferred that his wife should be safe from temptation.

We hired three donkeys, two for ourselves and one for our goods, the pots, kettle, bags of rice, flour, dried shark, onions, and Maria Theresa dollars which were always the heaviest item of luggage. Our party was completed by the owners of the donkeys, two beduin, a serious minded man called Muhammad of the Samuh tribe, and his more lighthearted companion, also called Muhammad, but of the Ba Haq tribe. Both had long, curly ringlets and each wore a short dark blue cotton *futa* held up by a belt from which a curved, sheathed dagger stood out prominently, a useful implement for cutting anything from meat to strips of leather for making sandals. Neither beduin carried a gun, the first time I had ever travelled with unarmed beduin. This was a quite remarkable event and a sure sign of the success of the peace throughout the country.

It had been raining heavily the night before we left which made us all cheerful as it meant there would be plentiful fodder for the donkeys; indeed at the first village we reached the men had all gone off to the hills to bring back fresh green fodder and we found only a few women, among them the mother of our companion, Muhammad Ba Haq, who was tending goats near a pool in which her daughter was washing her long black hair. The mother looked at least sixty but was probably no more than forty or so; the continuous open air life in the blazing sun gave beduin a lined, weather-beaten look at an early age, and they had responsibilities laid on them when still so young that they rarely seemed to have a childhood. A beduin boy would be wearing a dagger and learning the lore of camel tracks at an age when a town lad started school, and a beduin girl would be taking a handful of dates to go walking alone for miles with a herd of goats when a girl of the same age living in the shelter of a harem was still looked on as a baby.

One of the pleasant moments on journeys such as this was sitting round the fire drinking coffee after a good evening meal of rice and dried shark. It was then that the beduin talked about themselves, their lives, their love affairs, their feuds, and sometimes their poetry and their traditions. Life for them was to a large extent uncomplicated. Having survived infancy their pattern of life was like the landscape that surrounded them, simple as the desert with no possibility of deviating from the narrow winding tracks that the feet of their forefathers had made. They grew to manhood accustomed to hardship, believing in a God who knew what was best for them, and even if they were driven abroad through hunger or poverty to earn money, they retained their supreme confidence in their natural superiority as Arabs of the desert. Pride of clan or tribe was also strong and they inherited traditions and taboos, the origins of which were lost in the past. There were the various ways in which women spoke of their husbands; if they were asked their names someone else must reply for them as it was unlucky to say your own name. There was an almost universal taboo on a woman milking a camel, and there were certain words or phrases which men of a particular tribe must not use. I remember sitting round a camp fire listening to the men trying in every way to make the beduin who held the coffee pot use the word for 'pour out', knowing that in his case this was a taboo word. Another might not say 'monkey', and there were many more such taboo words. Our two Muhammads told Salih and me that beduin had a foreknowledge of events to come, citing as evidence the expressions used by them in bygone times which had meaning many years later; expressions such as, 'fly in the air to Qishn', used long before there were aeroplanes, or, 'I'll have a gun that takes five', when they were still using flintlocks. Today, they told us, the common expression is, 'The beduin will be empty', meaning that in the years to come the motor car would take away their livelihood.

On the first day after leaving Mukalla we crossed the coastal plain westwards towards the hills on the other side of which lay Wadi Hajr. When we reached the foothills we followed a winding, rocky track to about 2,000 feet, spending a very cold night half way up the pass. In the early morning, in order to warm up, I continued climbing on foot. The stillness was absolute except for my plodding footsteps. Gradually the birds began to take an interest in the day, flitting from rocky boulder to scrubby thorn bush, and singing ever more cheerfully as the sun rose. Thin veils of cloud hung round the hillsides leaving wisps of grey clinging to the boulders, but by the time I had reached the top of the pass and had come out on to the plateau the sun was high in the sky, turning the dark peaks to a soft gold. I sat on a stony ledge to wait for the donkeys and watched mine as, with head lowered, he wound his way up the path, sure-footed but with such an air of patient resignation that I felt guilty as I added my weight to the cross that he, like all the other donkeys, always bore on his back.

We continued across the plateau and at midday, when the heat was unbearable, stopped in a shallow depression where a few thorn trees gave scant shade. An old woman was sitting under one of them with her son; they had already walked twenty miles that day and were on their way to a village another twenty miles farther on. Three women carrying loads of firewood on their heads joined the old woman, and I took some coffee and dates over to them, sitting for a while to hear their news. One of the younger women had been to Mogadishu with her husband who earned his living there as an itinerant coffee-seller. Unlike townswomen, tribeswomen quite often went abroad with their husbands, which at least gave the man no excuse for taking another wife, as so often happened when the men emigrated alone. Tribeswomen were much freer in every way than townswomen; they were often unveiled and far more at ease in the company of men, sharing more fully their husbands' lives, yet in some ways they were treated with less respect than their more well-to-do sisters. For example, a tribesman would never demean himself by kissing the hand of any woman other than his mother's, and even then only after she had kissed his hand, while townsmen kissed their mothers' hands and heads, and the hands of their elder sisters or older women relatives.

All beduin were tribesmen but not all tribesmen were called beduin. The true *bedu* was a nomad, with no shelter but a cave or a tree where he was born, made love, and died, though he might sometimes have a stick hut in a village. The more affluent tribesmen who owned land, such as the Ja'adis in Wadi Amd, were not called *bedu*.

Beduin earned their livelihood by carrying goods or passengers on their donkeys and camels, while the women grazed the goats. Their life was one of hard work, little food, and endless walking. I have never known people walk so far to gain so little, miles and miles for a bundle of firewood or a skinful of water.

Towards evening we came to Yuwan, an area lying on the plateau that comprised a number of small villages. At the first one we were greeted in a friendly way and invited into the house of the head man, a two-storeyed mud brick house that looked prosperous compared to the hovels surrounding it. I was an object of much interest to the women who sat round the walls of the upstairs room allotted to me, staring in wonder as I washed, combed my hair, and changed my dress. What they found most extraordinary was the softness of my hands and feet which were stroked by each one in turn.

Men came in from other houses with numerous complaints for the 'Mustashar' (Adviser). They shook hands all round, sat with their backs to the wall, and we began with the usual preliminaries: 'Welcome – how are you? What news?' The answer was always, 'Praise be to God all is well,' followed usually by a catalogue of misfortunes. That evening there was one whose camel had been stolen and he wanted to know how he was to get it back without breaking the truce; a slave said he had been turned out of the house left him by his late master; my host complained that the soldiers billeted in the village used his house as if it were their own, they had even locked one of the principal rooms and had gone off with the key; someone else asked me to write a letter in English to a relation in India, and everyone wanted to have news of 'Ingrams' and the peace.

In the morning our host brought in a delicious breakfast of millet bread and honey, after which we set off again, leaving the plateau to follow dry water courses down to Wadi Hajr. There was not much to be seen except rocks and grey-green bushes, but as we came nearer to the wadi the water must have been close to the surface as the ground became greener and the bushes more flourishing. We could see the sunlight shining on the narrow strip of water on the far side of the valley and soon we were riding among date palms and occasional patches of green millet. We stayed the night in another village in the house of Abdulla the silversmith, which was not very clean so I hastily took off my glasses, on the principle that what the eye does not see the heart will not grieve over. Many of the women in this village spoke Swahili, having been to East Africa with their husbands, and it was a relief to find travelled women for they were only too pleased to air their knowledge of Christians, saving me a lot of trouble explaining the colour of my skin and hair. The women of Hajr were extremely pretty with small noses, wide full lips and broad

foreheads, but the young marrieds disguised their charms –
for me at least – by painting the upper half of their faces yellow and the lower half green.

When we left next day Salih, a slave, who had a complaint
and wanted a word in private, walked with us. During the
lunch halt he told his story. He had been freed but he was
married to a slave, Halima, who belonged to one Sheikh
Salim who had only allowed her to be married on condition
that half her children should belong to him. Salih and
Halima had two sons and they wanted to keep them both,
but Halima's master was trying to make her give up one of
them and had hit her on the head with a stone, beating her
until neighbours dragged them apart. As a law had recently
been passed in both the Qu'aiti and Kathiri states that
allowed slaves who wished to be free to obtain manumission,
I told Salih to take his wife to Mukalla where she would be
freed.

When this law had become known there was no wild rush
for freedom, just a trickle of men and women who had been
ill treated or who wished to try for work elsewhere, and as
freedom sometimes resulted in having no work and no means
of support, Harold arranged for those who applied for manumission to obtain work in Aden, and on the first occasion that
a number of men set sail from Mukalla I was travelling by
the same ship. The Aden Government was startled by a tele-
gram sent by one of the Mukalla clerks reading: 'Mrs
Ingrams with seven slaves arriving by S.S. Velho.'

Our second night in Wadi Hajr was spent at Kanina where
we stayed in a house perched on a rock with a fine view of the
other mud houses that lay close packed on the banks of the
wadi. Much of the land was ploughed up and in the early
morning I looked down from my eyrie on a peaceful scene at
a time when the light makes the country seem so soft and
beguiling, unlike the harshness it takes on in the heat of the
day. The sound of a boy singing rose clear and crisp. He was
urging on a laden donkey, the only living creatures in sight at
that hour, but by the time we were ready to leave the village
had come to life and swarms of children ran after us calling,

'Wife of Ingrams,' or, in more precise translation, 'Ingrams woman.'

Clouds gathered as we rode along the side of the wadi ie the afternoon and presently there was thunder and lightniny followed by a heavy downpour. We took shelter in a cave where we found a number of men and women also sheltering. The men lit a fire and took turns at puffing at a hookah, while the women stared at me wide-eyed, suckling their babies or rocking them gently in rush cradles. When the storm had cleared we rode on to our first close view of the perennial river. It was beautiful to see, the water reflecting the thick mass of date palms and the bright green patches of cultivation on either bank. I was just thinking that there was no lovelier sight in Arabia than running water when we heard shouts and a dull, roaring sound. We ran to the edge of the bank and saw a wall of flood-water stretching across to the other side and moving at great speed. Date trees and great branches of the *ariata* trees, bobbing about like some tormented beasts, were being whirled along, and it was easy to understand how people were drowned in these sudden floods for had we been at the edge of the river bed it would have been impossible to escape.

As we could go no farther until the waters subsided we spent the night under an overhanging cliff on the bank, and it was not long before men from a nearby village came to talk and air their complaints. When I had taken down all their statements they curled up on the rocks and stayed to spend the night with us. In the morning we saw that the water had risen to twelve feet but had now subsided to about two feet so we were able to wade across to the other side, leading the donkeys, and continue on our way, our clothes drying as we rode along. We had to ford the river once again but this time it was deep and running fast. The water was up to my shoulders and had it not been for the strong hand of a Yafa'i soldier who had joined us, I would have been swept off my feet.

We passed through several villages, with only the most primitive hovels made of sticks, that belonged to Subians, the

G

poorest of the agricultural labourers who as a class were despised by all other classes. It was they who supplied the men to clean out the 'long drops' in the towns, but here in Wadi Hajr they were reasonably content, particularly since the peace, which had meant that they could cultivate their land without the local tribesmen pouring kerosene on to their date palms. That evening we came to the farthest point of our journey, a village where Atif, the officer in charge of Hajr province, lived. He had been appointed by the Qu'aiti Government to develop agriculture, to tighten up control on customs on people coming from the Wahidi country in the west, and generally to keep order, but he was a local man subject to local intrigues and just before our arrival he had received a message from the State Secretary recalling him to Mukalla to answer charges of oppression. In spite of this he was all smiles and spoke a great deal of all the wonderful things he had done for the province. His cronies nodded agreement, but others approached me later when I was alone to complain about him.

When I was allowed to forget local politics I enjoyed our stay in this village in which all the houses had been built high and narrow, with slits for windows – a sign of how unsettled the area had been. As stone was available the buildings were of flat slabs that fitted one above the other and were wedged together by mud mixed with straw. The men of this village were unusually fat, due to their habit of drinking vast quantities of a brew made from the sap of the *asaf* palm. I was brought some for breakfast, all frothy and newly taken from the tree and poured into a plaited straw cup. Atif assured me it was not intoxicating if drunk before noon, therefore it was lawful for a Muslim to drink it in the morning. It tasted like a mixture of Italian vermouth and beer, slightly warm, and quite definitely intoxicating.

Wadi Hajr was remarkable among the provinces of Hadhramaut not only for its perennial water but because it had more date palms than anywhere else. The date harvest must have been a wonderful sight. On the outskirts of every village there were open spaces covered with pebbles on which the

dates were laid out to dry, and during the harvest the surrounding fields were filled with the camps of hundreds of
Yemenis, Adenis, and others from distant parts who came
with goods or money to exchange for them.

Apart from dates there was no other cash crop, but there
was no doubt about the possibility of cultivating more land,
providing the money could be found to do so. There was now
peace among the different tribes and the essential water was
there, but it would need money to build dams to stop the
flood water pouring into the sea and taking much of the top-
soil with it, and also to obtain agricultural advice as to the
best crops to grow. The prospects, however, were sufficiently
promising for Harold later on to start developing the Meifa
delta where the waters of Wadi Hajr ran into the sea, but
although a fertile area the cultivation was handicapped by
the prevalence of malaria and one of the first works under-
taken was the improvement of the drainage of the land.
Advances were made to the farmers to buy manure, guano
from islands nearby being used extensively, and small dams
were built to keep back at least some of the water, but this
was only one of many projects which would benefit the people
of South Arabia and there never was enough money either
from the local Treasuries or from the British Government to
finance all the things that needed to be done to improve conditions in the country. It can be argued, why should the
British taxpayer have paid for the people of South Arabia
who could give nothing in return? But it can also be argued
that if this were so, should we not have given up our 'protection' and allowed the people to look elsewhere for help?

Chapter 10

ARABS IN SINGAPORE AND JAVA

Emigration was vital to the Hadhramis in order to compensate for the difficulty of making a livelihood at home by sending remittances from abroad. Those who went to East Africa rarely made fortunes, those who went to Hyderabad sometimes did rather better, but the wealthiest Hadhramis were those who emigrated to Singapore and Java. They not only supported numerous relatives at home in comparative luxury, but indirectly gave work to builders, craftsmen, agricultural labourers, and the beduin who carried their goods from the coast to the inland towns. Therefore any falling off of remittances from the East Indies could result in hardship to thousands of Hadhramis who had no direct connection with the islands. The money sent home was not always put to good use, it sometimes helped to keep up tribal wars. Families such as the Buqris or the Bin Abdats had amassed fortunes from business ventures in Java and continued to wage war on their enemies, even when they were abroad, by sending money home to buy arms. In 1939 there were about 80,000 Hadhramis in the East Indies whose strong ties with their homelands made them follow events there with the greatest attention. As there was a great deal of speculation about 'Ingrams' Peace', as it was called, and the developments that had taken place since Harold had become Adviser – the organizing of better administration, the training of the armed forces, the building of roads, and the development of educational and medical services – he decided to visit the Arabs in Singapore and Java to tell them what was happening in the Hadhramaut and enlist their moral and financial support. He also arranged to visit the Unfederated Malay States to study their treaties and their administration with a view to adapting anything that might be useful to the Hadhramaut.

Leaving Zahra in our house in Aden in the care of a friend, Harold and I set sail via Aden and Ceylon for Singapore. The Governor, Sir Shenton Thomas, offered us hospitality at Government House, a magnificent building in the true imperial tradition. It had the highest rooms I had ever seen and I thought that even if we took no other exercise we would get enough simply walking about the house. The Thomas's were far less imperial than their surroundings, indeed Sir Shenton was the first and only governor I ever saw sitting in the front seat of the gubernatorial car with his driver. During our stay, Admiral Sir Percy Noble, who was Commander-in-Chief East Indies, arrived for a conference with a party of French brass hats, for the threat of war was already a considerable cloud on the horizon.

Leaving Singapore we went north to the Unfederated State of Kelantan where the Resident, Mr Baker, was much troubled by the Japanese infiltration along the coast on the pretext of tin mining or fishing. He felt sure that if it came to war with Japan they would quite easily be able to land at Bachok, a seaside resort where the Bakers had a bungalow, and also capture the airstrip which, in spite of his warnings, was unprotected. He was later proved right on both counts.

Harold made a study of the administrations of Kelantan, Trengganu, Perlis, and Kedah, after which we stayed for a few days in Kuala Lumpur where he had talks with officials, and then we returned to Singapore. Whilst staying in Alor Star, the capital of Kedah, the Resident gave a dinner party in honour of General and Mrs Dobbie. The General was making a farewell tour prior to retirement and no one ever imagined that in only a year or two he would be Governor of Malta during its most critical war years. Nor could we have imagined the tragedy and horrors that were to overtake many of our hosts and friends in Malaya when the country was overrun by the Japanese three years later.

On our return to Singapore we stayed in a house on Mount Washington lent to us by the Al Kaf family, which had the most glorious views from a window that went right across one side of the house. Here Harold could start writing his report and I could do the typing. I also took the opportunity of meeting as many of the Malay families of Hadhrami men as I could, struggling along in halting Malay as few of the women spoke Arabic. Here was the other side of the coin – they were the second families of the men I had known in the Hadhramaut, men who spent some years at home with their Hadhrami family, then took their turn in running the Singapore business, returning after a few years with perhaps one or two sons of the Malay wife, whom they wanted brought up in an Arabic-speaking country. I met a number of mothers anxious to have news of their sons still in the Hadhramaut, just as many women in the Hadhramaut has asked me to meet their husbands, sons, or brothers when I was in the East Indies. It was pleasant to see how free the Malay wives were, walking out in their sarongs with no outdoor cloaks, or taking a car without curtained windows to visit their friends. Their daughters, unlike girls in the Hadhramaut, went to school and even if they were unlikely to take up a career they at least had some education before being married at fifteen or sixteen.

We had a constant stream of Arab visitors at the house on Mount Washington, and Harold had to speak on Hadhrami affairs at numerous tea and dinner parties. Some Arab residents were suspicious about the intentions of the British Government in the Hadhramaut and among the prominent personalities who voiced doubts was Seiyid Ibrahim Al Saqqaf, head of the Saqqaf family, which was as wealthy and as important as the Al Kafs. Ibrahim was then in his late thirties, quiet in manner with a rather delicate air, but he was active in business and in journalism and took a keen interest in the Hadhramaut although he had never been there, having been born and brought up in Mecca. He put forward ideas for the formation of a company among emigrant Hadhramis to promote the welfare of their homeland, agriculturally and through the development of trade, but he also expressed the fears of many of his compatriots that the British would try to run the Hadhramaut on what he called

'African lines', meaning as a colony under direct rule. It was interesting to see how he and his supporters gradually became less suspicious as Harold outlined his ideas for the development of the country in its own Arab way with its own Arab leaders, and with only a handful of British technicians so long as this was necessary. Some became enthusiastic for British assistance, one voiced a wish to see a British Commonwealth of Nations extending to all Arab and Muslim countries, another wanted self-government in close alliance with the British. It seems strange now to recall such attitudes, but they were men living under a well run British administration in Singapore and the wind of change was but a gentle zephyr in 1939.

From Singapore we went by boat to Batavia and after staying there a few days, meeting many Arab emigrés, we crossed Java by car calling at Cheribon, Tegal, Pekalongen, and Solo, on our way to Surabaya. The Dutch authorities were extremely helpful all through our visit to Java, arranging the tour so that we could meet as many Arabs as possible, and in particular the Governor of East Java, Mr von der Platz, was interested in the Arab communities as he had served as Consul in Jedda. In each town the Arabs formed a large well-organized community under a headman, and everywhere we went there were deputations and receptions to meet Harold, who had to make speech after speech in Arabic. During the receptions I would go behind the scenes to meet the families and exchange news of relatives, for although the women were semi-emancipated they did not mix with the men at public functions. It was rare to find any woman who had come from the Hadhramaut, and when I did meet one I found she never had the same longing for it as the men, who, in spite of the modern, sophisticated lives they led in Java, always spoke nostalgically of their beloved wadis. Seeing them sitting behind imposing desks in smart suits it was difficult to believe these were the same men we had seen in *futas* on the floors of mud houses. One of them, a warlike chief in his own country, was transformed into the tycoon owner of one of the best hotels in Batavia with a Dutch manager obsequiously attending to his orders, another owned a large factory, yet a third had a chain of shops.

It was not events in the Hadhramaut alone that occupied the attention of the Hadhramis in Java in 1939, for not only were they Hadhramis but they were also Arabs and anything that affected the Arab world affected them. Harold was constantly asked about Palestine and what the British Government's intentions were towards Arabs and Jews: there were even some who expressed the fear that the new interest being taken by the British in the Hadhramaut was because they intended to settle Jews there as well as in Palestine.

It was a fascinating although exhausting tour – we slept in twenty different beds in less than two months – and we gained an insight into what lay behind the wealth of certain Hadhrami families and why it was so important to the Hadhramaut to maintain this East Indies connection. We only stayed a few days in Singapore after returning from Java and then took a ship to India, where we were to stay in Hyderabad, first with the Resident, and then with the Qu'aiti Sultan who was visiting his estates there. However we had only been four or five days in Hyderabad when Harold was recalled to Aden. It was then the 23rd of August and war was imminent. Three days later we caught the P. & O. liner from Bombay and the captain broadcast to the passengers on the first day at sea that he was now under Admiralty orders, that he hoped he would be able to deliver us all safely to our destinations; he told us to keep calm, to put up with inconveniences, and to use as little fresh water as possible in case the ship had to be diverted. Lounges and cabins were blacked out and boat drill was frequent. When we reached Aden on the 31st the harbour had taken on a wartime look with destroyers, a cruiser and a submarine awaiting orders.

We remained in Aden only long enough to collect supplies and, together with Zahra, took the first available boat to Mukalla, the ancient tub *Africa*, which always surprised me by keeping afloat, and it was while we were aboard her that we heard war had been declared.

Chapter Eleven

WORLD WAR AND LOCAL PEACE

When we returned to Mukalla from the East Indies there was more work than ever; the war meant a number of new regulations which had to be enforced including the censorship of letters. Every morning Muhammad Ba Matraf, the Residency interpreter, and I sat down to large batches of letters addressed to East Africa, India, Aden, or the East Indies. They were sad letters, mostly written on behalf of women whose husbands had left them penniless and to soften the heart of an errant husband they often included the footprint of a child he had perhaps never seen; but the letters were unlikely to be of interest to an enemy, though just occasionally there were remarks about local events which had to be cut out.

Apart from censorship, new measures to deal with supplies and other wartime inconveniences, it was advisable to keep everyone as informed as possible about the progress of the war so a local broadcasting station was set up with help from Aden and loud speakers placed in the market square where the men gathered in the evenings to drink coffee. The broadcasts were a great asset to the coffee shops, whose trade increased tenfold, and each evening you could see groups of men listening intently to the relay of the B.B.C. Arabic Service, which was the main source of news and which quickly gained a high reputation.

As 1939 came to an end Hadhramis were growing more concerned about their home affairs than about the war in Europe since 1940 would see the end of the three years' truce. Unless it could be extended there was a real possibility of a return to the internecine war that had previously stultified all chance of development. Harold had already begun a campaign to extend the truce for ten years and, as part of the publicity, I set off on a journey to the Bursheid and Deiyin tribes who were known to be ready to start fighting again, and whose distant territory in the north-west neither of us had yet visited. A middle-aged seiyid, Hasan bin Muhammad, went with me. His home was in the heart of Deiyin country where he had been accustomed to using his influence as a seiyid to keep the peace. We were a small party, Hasan, myself, and two beduin, one of them from the Bursheid tribe, a sturdy man called Awadh who was always protesting his willingness to help in every way but in fact did as little as he could, and Salim of the Samuh tribe, one that seemed to produce quiet, gentle, thoughtful beduin, for I had been fortunate in travelling with Samuh tribesmen before and they all got on with the job without fuss and were among the most pleasant of companions.

We had three donkeys, one for Hasan, one for me, and one for our goods. In my diary I made a list of the luggage for this trip: 1 camp bed, 3 rugs, 2 Arab pillows (these were long and hard), 1 overcoat, change of clothes, S.Ts, powder, toothbrush, etc., cigarettes, matches, notebooks, pencils, large saucepan, small saucepan, serving spoon, 2 enamel plates, mug, canvas water bottle, kettle, lantern, torch. The disposal of sanitary towels was always a problem on the stony plateaux, and the best I could ever do was to scratch a hole and bury them under a heap of stones. These memorial cairns were to be found all over the deserts of the Hadhramaut. As for other natural functions it was not easy to perform them unseen when there was not a rock nor a tree in sight for miles, so I followed the example of the ostrich and, having walked a good distance from the camp, turned my back on it, satisfied that if I could not see the beduin they could not see me.

We started off up the – by now familiar – road to Du'an, meeting a number of caravans with men emigrating to East Africa as it was the migrating season when the monsoon would blow them to Mombasa. Among them was a large caravan from Deiyin and the tribesmen were interested to hear that we were on the way to their country, describing it as still several days away. When travelling by camel or donkey we reckoned distance in hours or days, never in miles. After some hours on the road to Du'an we turned off, taking a track that led towards the north west. It was new country to me but appeared no different from the more familiar areas, as it was all part of the same plateau, and we continued winding round low hills or deep ravines, tediously following the whitened track of centuries which like an unending snake stretched for miles across the stones. Tribes living on the plateaux have settlements that extend for several miles and comprise a number of small villages, which are known by the name of the tribe. The first such settlement that we reached belonged to the tribe of our beduin, Awadh of the Bursheid, and we spent the night in a hut made of sticks that had been speedily cleaned out for us, after which the entire population crowded into it.

I had been given a supply of printed notices describing how the three years' truce was to be extended for ten years and handed some round but few could read, so Hasan and I did what we could to explain what they said. Wherever we stopped on this journey I found that perhaps one man in the village could read and he would be called upon to read aloud to the others, but no one was used to print, nor to the grammatical Arabic of the text, and Seiyid Hasan and I had to interpret. The tribesmen would nod their heads in agreement or click their tongues against their teeth to show disapproval, and there was always someone to ask awkward questions.

On this first night I was asked what the Government would do about goats that were stolen if people were not going to be allowed to retaliate. I replied that they should lock up their goats at night and if, as they said, stealing was frequent they should set a guard instead of shutting themselves up in their huts, adding censoriously that they could not expect Government to do everything for them if they could not help themselves to this extent. One man brought up a case of camel stealing that had occurred two years before, storming at me, 'I have been waiting for the three years truce to end so that I may loot their camels and now Government wants me to wait another ten years, that's not good enough.' In the next village I was asked what would happen if someone stole or killed and there were no witnesses, for Government, they said, would do nothing without witnesses. I told them that the men of the newly formed Hadhrami Beduin Legion would look into such cases, saying priggishly that they must themselves give what help they could. I was becoming quite a schoolmarm as I warmed to the job.

Awadh's home was in the largest of the Bursheid villages, some distance from our first night's halt, and we spent the second night in his house. He was obviously a prosperous man as it was built of mud bricks and three storeys high. The stairs to the top room which he put at my disposal were as grimy as all the well-worn mud stairs that I had trodden in so many different villages, but my room was well swept and the walls clean. There was only one window, shuttered against the cold night air, for it was winter and we were some 3000 feet above sea level, but I threw open the wooden shutters (there were never any panes of glass) and sat breathing in the fresh air as more women crowded into the room. They were unveiled and without shyness in front of the men, nor did they maul me as several of them had been to East Africa and did not find me particularly strange. I found the women everywhere strongly in favour of continuing the peace. Tribal feuds meant to them the killing or wounding of their husbands and brothers, and they could see no sense in living in a state of continual anxiety, but they had little or no influence over the men when it came to a question of tribal pride and retaliating in the traditional way.

These tribal villages were much poorer than those in Wadi Du'an or Wadi Amd, and except for the few who had mud houses most of the inhabitants lived in stick huts. There were no 'long drops' and washing was done in a room with a hole in one corner through which the water ran out on to the ground outside. Awadh's daughter took me by the hand to show me the local 'ladies', a piece of wasteland surrounded by a broken down wall, some two hundred yards away, where all the women gathered when the need arose. The distance we had to walk reminded me of the time I was with a theatrical touring company in Sheffield. I had asked my landlady for the lavatory. She took a key from a hook in the kitchen, led me through the back door, along an alleyway into another street where, behind a fence, there was a row of six earth closets for the use of two streets.

As these journeys by camel or donkey took on a similar pattern each day was much alike. The entries in my diary, written in pencil and with no attempt at style, convey something of the country and the people as they struck me at that moment in time:

Monday, 1st January. New Year's Day and I seem to be out of this world in a timeless existence. Awadh's daughter Fatima brought me hard boiled eggs, coffee, and freshly made wheat bread which we ate together. It took some time to say goodbye because Awadh lingered with last instructions for his family. Also Hasan and I had a crowd round us asking whether Government would really take any action if someone broke the truce. Several men pointed to a mud fort on a hill saying they wanted five soldiers there to keep the peace.

About an hour after leaving we came to some stick and mud huts surrounded by thorn trees and were asked to stay, but felt we must push on. It was bitterly cold owing to a biting north east wind, more like England than Arabia. I've worn a jersey all day long every day which shows how cold it is, even at midday. We rode through a number of other villages where men, women and children ran after us to see the stranger and shake our hands. Finally we halted for lunch at Arum where we were taken to the communal hut, which was pitch black after the sunlight, and it took some time for my eyes to become accustomed to the change of light. We drank coffee and talked about peace until lunch came, bread, soup, boiled meat and rice.

Seiyid Ali the Bedui joined us from Wadi Amd (some distance away to the north) during the afternoon. There were many more villages and at each one we dismounted to talk to the Muqaddam (headman). I always make sure Seiyid Hasan rides ahead as I know it would greatly offend his dignity if a woman were to ride in front of him when we come to a village. He, for his part, always insists wherever we stay for the night that I should be given a clean room with no bugs. No one ever takes offence.

Tuesday, 2nd January. Nijeidin. It was still dark when the old headman of Nijeidin banged on my door wanting a kettle from the room, probably to do his ablutions before the dawn prayer. I got up soon afterwards, packed up my bed and made room on the floor for us to breakfast. We got away soon after seven and were followed all day by an old man whose legs were so bowed I feared they would give way all together. Wherever he went he got free meals and a corner to sleep, so I suppose he will go on wandering until he finally collapses.

Last night an elderly man wanted to know if Government would let him find thieves for them as he had the power of seeing anyone who had committed a crime by looking into a bowl of water. I told him I was afraid Government might not take this as reliable evidence. Others present protested that Government always wanted witnesses to a crime, whereas they thought the tribal custom of trial by ordeal more successful.

Wednesday, 3rd January, Lakhshab. Last night I had a long talk with the headman who said he would write to 'Ingrams' about the Deiyin hostages who were being held by the Ba Surras in Wadi Du'an and who, according to him, were not being properly fed. He also had much to say about the squabbles between the different Deiyin clans. I felt very tired with so much talk and rather feverish. The women, few of them in this house, brought incense which warmed me. They came again after dinner and I had to put up the camp bed as they had never seen one before and all wanted to try sitting on it.

The Deiyin country is full of villages so our progress has been slow. At one village the headman refused to take the peace notices. He was quite young, suspicious, obstinate and truculent. He said he would rather the tribesmen took the law into their own hands unless Government would restore looted goods. In this village I felt that no one was in favour of the ten years extension as they were anxiously awaiting the end of the three years truce to carry on their feuds. We argued with them for four hours and parted friends but with little satisfaction on either side.

Tribesmen are notoriously independent-minded and the Deiyin were no exception. They lived a long way from settled administration and found the *Dola*, or Government, slow to make decisions, therefore they preferred taking the law into their own hands, robbing those who robbed them, to waiting for 'justice' from an apparently indifferent government. The Deiyin were nominally subject to the Qu'aiti Sultan of Shihr and Mukalla and came under the jurisdiction of the governors of Du'an province, the Ba Surra brothers, who tried to maintain order among the tribes by the traditional method of taking hostages. The regular Qu'aiti forces were quite insufficient to deal with tribal disturbances but Harold had already created the Hadhrami Beduin Legion, recruited from the tribes and trained to deal with tribesmen as soldiers, police and arbitrators. However it was still a young force though it was hoped that it would eventually be strong enough to assist in seeing that a ten years extension to the truce was maintained.

Leaving Deiyin country we turned northwards towards Wadi Amd, reaching the pass from the plateau to the wadi at the hottest time of the day. The pass was so steep that it was believed a saintly Sheikh finding no path down the cliffs to the valley struck the rocks with his stick, splitting them and forming a narrow passage. We took over an hour to get ourselves and the donkeys down, perspiring from the heat that rose from the valley, and no sooner were we in the valley than we were enveloped by flies, agreeably absent from the colder villages on the plateau. It was dark when we came to Amd, the town where I had stayed with the man from Java. This time he was living alone, having sent his wife and daughter back to Java, which must have been a great relief to them as they had hated the life in the Hadhramaut. I was given their quarters and in the morning found that my host had locked me in, no doubt for my own protection.

The Ja'adis had signed the three years' truce, and had kept it, but I found that in some cases they were waiting impatiently for it to end so that they could continue their feuds. Most of those I met, however, were well content and glad at the prospect of ten years more peace. I stayed two nights in Wadi Amd before reaching Hureidha, one of them with the mother-in-law of Alawi al Attas whom I found searching through a bundle of clothes for a winding sheet, as an infant girl had been stillborn to her son's wife an hour before we arrived. The father was quite unperturbed, so was grandmother, but then children were so easy to come by and so many died in infancy that hearts were barely moved. They just said, 'It is the will of God'.

At Hureidha I said goodbye to Seiyid Hasan whose help had been invaluable in arguing with the difficult Deiyin. I was not at all sure that we had been successful in pointing out the benefits of peace and indeed it was not until some time later, when the Hadhrami Beduin Legion was proving a success, that they finally agreed to join in the ten years' peace.

Two of the Attas family took me by car to Shibam, where we stopped to meet the Indian doctor who had recently been engaged to start a clinic there, a much needed and much appreciated appointment. His clinic was crowded with patients and his enthusiasm refreshing. When one had seen so many people suffering needlessly through lack of treatment, it was a relief to feel that at least some sufferers would now have the benefit of medical attention and the chance of being cured.

I spent a night in Seiyun with Fatima and her family and gave them news of their relations in the East Indies, then went on to Tarim where, in Sheikha's house, I relived our days in Singapore as she and her mother were anxious to hear every detail about their families, their friends, and the island. There was a newcomer in the harem, a lovely, sophisticated girl called Lulu who had married Sheikha's eldest son, Sheikh,

Forced landing. 'Zahra showed her adaptability in any circumstances.' (Ch. 8)

Women walk miles for a bundle of firewood or a skinful of water

Our house in Mukalla beflagged for the coronation of George VI

Mukalla

when he was studying dentistry in Cairo. Lulu's father was a Hadhrami seiyid who had gone to live in Egypt where Lulu had been born and brought up, so that the Hadhramaut was even more foreign to her than it was to me. Her short skirts made it difficult for her to sit on the floor and she could not bring herself to eat with her fingers, but worst of all was the seclusion in which she found herself. She could not go out with her husband, or at all unless she wore the Hadhrami cloak and veil, which she refused to do, so she spent her time in a large room furnished thoughtfully by her father-in-law with bed, tables and chairs. Lulu was fond of her parents-in-law but she could not adapt herself to their way of life, although she found great kindness among the household who did their best to make her happy. When I arrived she was in a very worried state of mind because she was nearly seven months pregnant and not unnaturally terrified at the thought of having a baby in a place where there was neither doctor nor midwife. Her husband Sheikh was equally worried because he could not get her away as there had been trouble among tribes living near the motor road to the coast and the route was closed. I promised to ask Harold to do what he could to help them.

Meanwhile I had another donkey ride ahead of me, this time along a route new to me, the Wadi Bin Ali, which runs into Wadi Hadhramaut from the south. We – four beduin, two camels for the luggage and a donkey for me – were to follow the wadi to its source, then cross the plateau and down to the coastal plain, a distance of about a hundred miles. Wadi Bin Ali was dry and sparsely inhabited and most of those we met were coming from Mukalla with camels laden with goods for the towns in Wadi Hadhramaut. We made good progress, with short halts and long rides, to the point where the wadi narrowed and we had to climb the ravine that led to the plateau. By then the sun was setting so we halted near the top of the pass, the beduin lit a fire and cooked rice with dried shark which we all ate out of the pot. There were no shelters on this route, as it was not commonly used by travellers, and our nights were spent in the open air,

H

but as we rode for ten or eleven hours each day I was too weary to care where I laid my head. Such long rides were unusual, as beduin like to travel in the early morning and have a long halt during the heat of the day, then move on again until sunset, but it was now winter and they felt no need for a long rest in the middle of the day. 'There is no sun' they assured me. Perhaps they did not feel its heat, though my sunburnt arms and face told a different story, but it was more tiring to argue than to agree, and I was by now only too anxious to finish the journey and get back to the routine of life in Mukalla. From the flat tableland we gradually descended to the coastal plain and on the sixth day saw in the distance the date palms of Gheil Ba Wazir, a large town set among cultivation and famed for its tobacco, grown and dried locally, and sent to Mukalla for export. Water was plentiful and there were banana palms, lime trees, and sweet potatoes in abundance. It was as if we had come into another world and I appreciated why the Arabs say that the best things in life are running water, green fields, and a pretty woman – in that order.

Chapter Twelve

INTERLUDE IN EGYPT

When I got back I told Harold about the problem of Lulu's baby and he asked the R.A.F. to bring her and Sheikh to Mukalla as a friendly gesture. They stayed a few days with us before taking a ship to Aden where they waited in our house for another ship to Egypt, arriving at Lulu's home two days before her baby was born. We had all become very friendly and I gladly accepted their invitation to stay with them in Cairo for the birth of our baby which I was expecting in a few months' time. Harold had been appointed Chief Secretary to the Aden Government so this meant leaving him to wind up not only his office work but also the household.

It was not without misgivings that we left Mukalla. There had been so many new developments in the Hadhramaut since we had first made it our home, developments in medical and educational services, in agriculture, in communications, in the armed forces, and in general administration, but there was still much to be done. However, as Chief Secretary, Harold would be able to keep an eye on progress in the Hadhramaut while extending his activities to the Western Aden Protectorate and to Aden itself.

Taking Zahra – now aged four – with me, I left Mukalla for Aden to wait there for a ship to Suez. We had to be ready to leave the house at a moment's notice, for wartime secrecy prevented our knowing ships' movements. Word came early one afternoon that we should be at the quayside in half an hour to take passage in a cargo ship, but though we were there on time we arrived only to see the ship steaming out of the harbour. Nothing daunted, the ship's agent somehow persuaded the man in charge of the signal gun to fire it and halt the ship. Meanwhile Zahra and I got into a motor-boat and were taken at great speed out to sea. The ship heaved to, dropped anchor and the gangway was lowered. It says much for the good temper of the captain that he made us welcome when, instead of an official bearing news of the Italian entry into the war which was what he expected when the gun was fired, a pregnant woman with a child came up the gangway.

I was not a stranger to Cairo but it was the first time I had stayed with an Egyptian family. Seiyid Hasan al Bar, Lulu's father, came from Wadi Du'an and had married a Hadhrami girl who had been born in Egypt and his own children were completely Egyptianized. Although Seiyid Hasan wore the Egyptian *galabieh* he retained a deep nostalgia for his Hadhrami valley and loved nothing better than to eat the simply cooked rice and boiled meat of the Hadhramaut, or the richer feast-day dishes of date purée eaten with ghee, or meat cooked in a porridge of millet flour. As he still talked in the Hadhrami dialect he was the one member of the family I could understand and who could understand me. It took me some time to get used to the Egyptian dialect.

I was fascinated to see the contrast between Hadhrami women in their homeland and those who lived in more sophisticated countries, for among the Al Bar friends were many Hadhrami families. The older women, like 'Mama' al Bar, belonged to the transition period between purdah and emancipation. 'Mama' did not veil but always wore black out of doors and carried a thin piece of black voile in her hand which could have veiled her face but was, in fact, just a concession to tradition and only waved about in the air. She had never in her life been in a restaurant until I persuaded her to have an iced coffee in Groppi's when she gazed around with that excited tremulous air of one indulging in forbidden fruits.

The household revolved round 'Papa' but when he was away visiting his cotton plantation at Heria, near Zagazig, it was Sheikh who deputized as head of the house. Sheikh was then in his twenties and had more or less decided to give up studying to be a dentist and instead to go into his father's business in Singapore. Though an able young man he had been used to a life of idleness in the Hadhramaut and found it a bore to concentrate on study. He was, however, anxious to show that he knew how a house should be run and that punctuality was not an eccentricity of Europeans but a necessary part of modern life, and during his father-in-law's absence decided that everyone should be at table ready for breakfast at half past eight; in future there should be no more turning up any time between eight and ten. The first morning after this edict we all obeyed his instructions and were sitting round the table as the clock struck, all, that is, except Sheikh who was fast asleep in bed.

The Al Bars lived in a ground floor flat in Abbassia, on the main street, so that when the windows of the front rooms were open the clanking trams, the cries of street sellers and the general noise of traffic, drowned conversation. It could not drown, however, the powerful voice of Um Kulthum, Egypt's most famous singer, whose lengthy songs poured out from the radio for many hours of the day and night. Still the most popular singer in the Arab world, this amazing woman, now in her sixties, continues to enthral thousands with songs that each last for several hours.

The flat was quite spacious. Sheikh, Lulu and their baby girl, Zeinab, occupied the front bedroom that led off the hall, which was used as the dining-room. On the other side of the hall was the parlour with hard, upright chairs and small tables, always kept clean and ready for the more formal visitors such as 'Papa's' business friends or those acquaintances who came to enquire after Lulu and her baby. We usually sat either in the hall-dining-room or the 'utility room' where the sewing and ironing was done. 'Papa' and 'Mama' had a bedroom at the back, another was shared by the three sons, and another by the two younger daughters, Su'ad and Fawzia. There were two bathrooms, western and eastern, the former used by all the family except 'Papa' who preferred to ladle water over himself rather than to lie in it. No servants lived in the flat, but Um Sabri, a large bosomed motherly woman, came to cook and clean, there was a young boy who went to the market or ran errands, and a man who came about once a week to do the ironing.

It was rather disconcerting at first when the boys, Ghazali,

Abdul Qadir and Hussein, changed into pyjamas the moment they returned from university or school, but I, too, quickly fell into the comfortable habit of walking around all day long in a housecoat. I saw little of Ghazali, the eldest, for as a university student he was out with his contemporaries most of the time. The second son, Abdul Qadir, was about fourteen and having difficulty with his examinations, so he was being given extra tuition during the holidays, much to his disgust. Hussein, the youngest, was full of mischief and had not yet reached the age when examinations were a serious obstacle and he was cheerful and happy-go-lucky. Both boys ran in and out of the house in their pyjamas, visiting friends or being sent on errands. Su'ad, their sister, a pretty plump girl of fifteen, did not care about school but had the makings of a good housewife and mother. She helped 'Mama' in the home and she took Zahra under her wing, playing with her like a pet doll, alternately scolding or kissing her, and I was grateful to have her to look after Zahra when it was time for me to go to the clinic for the birth of my baby.

Last but by no means least was Fawzia, then aged about ten, to my mind the prettiest of them all with her long, high cheekboned face which showed her Du'ani ancestry, her dark thoughtful eyes, and a brown skin that 'Mama' considered to be 'beduin' and less matrimonially attractive than the pale faces of Lulu and Su'ad. Fawzia had brains as well as beauty and I was not surprized to find, when I saw the family again in 1966, that she, like her brother Abdul Qadir, had become a doctor, combining medicine with bringing up a family.

This was the family that made Zahra and me welcome, and recalling it now I am amazed at their hospitality. Living in Arabia I had grown accustomed to the generous welcome we received everywhere, but now that I have been many years in England where front doors are always shut and an unknown visitor looked on with misgiving, I appreciate even more the warmth of the welcome the Al Bar family gave us.

When we arrived in Cairo Lulu's baby was a month old and very ill. Everything possible was being done for her, from calling in the doctor who attended the king's children to visiting the local saint, but it was no use and the child died when she was six months old. Lulu and Sheikh later went to live in Singapore where we saw them again in 1950 with a family of several daughters, but tragically Lulu was killed in a motor accident and when the family grew up Sheikh retired to his old home in Tarim in the Hadhramaut to live with his widowed mother, Sheikha.

Cairo was in the grip of war fever. There was grim news from Europe and the imminent possibility of the Italians coming into the war. Each evening Sheikh hired a car to take Lulu and me for a drive or we would walk along the banks of the Nile enjoying the cool air after the exhausting heat of a May day. Wherever we went we were acutely aware of the great number of British troops and as I knew of the resentment at the only too common attitude of the British to the 'wogs', it was refreshing to find that Su'ad at least was a fan of the British soldiers, because, as she told me, they gave up their seats to her in the trams. It was realized that Cairo would be within bombing range of the Italians if they came into the war and so 'Papa' thought it prudent for the entire family to prepare to move to their country home. The flat was filled with packing cases and 'Mama' wrote out lists of goods that she would have to buy to take to the primitive village of Heria. She proposed to take Zahra with them and I was to join them as soon as I could after our baby was born. This event was due to take place in a house belonging to Zalal Abdul Latif, the Egyptian midwife who had attended Lulu. She had been trained at the famous Kasr al Aini hospital and had her own clinic with a room for lying-in patients on the ground floor of her house. She lived above with her two sisters. They were Jews but Zalal's clientele was predominantly Muslim and there was the greatest friendliness between them all. This friendship was still strong in 1966 in spite of all that had happened in Palestine, but then Zalal and her sisters were Egyptians by nationality and Jews by religion only.

The day when the Italians did come into the war the Cairo

air-raid sirens sounded in a false alarm, and 'Mama's' excitable sister, Tante Fardus, came rushing round, enveloped all the children in her embrace and cried in a voice of doom 'Death, death, let us all die together'. Fortunately for everyone's peace of mind 'Mama' was more practical and having put the last nail into a packing case, sent off all the goods by lorry to Heria, and prepared to follow with the family a few days later. I was already living in Zalal's house, having had my personal false alarm, and the night before the family were to leave Cairo for the country Sheikh took 'Mama', Lulu and me to the theatre to see Yusuf Wahbi in a comedy. Early the next morning the baby started and when Zalal had to go out to another patient I began to panic in case she was not there at the crucial moment. I need not have worried for not only was she there, calm and unruffled, but also her sister Badia who held my hand while they both encouraged me with cries of 'Poussez'. Neither sister spoke a word of English, nor could they understand my Arabic so we usually talked in French: having a baby is difficult enough without the added complication of communicating in a foreign language. However soon after eleven in the morning Zalal held up a red-faced infant for my inspection 'wrapped in swaddling clothes'. Forgetting all about the Bible I was quite frantic, convinced that the child had no arms. It was only after Zalal had unwrapped all the bandages that I would believe I had a perfectly normal baby.

The Al Bar family were leaving for Heria that same morning but found time to bring Zahra round to see her sister. She was not impressed, having much more interesting things to talk about such as her journey to the country and all the things she was going to do there. I hoped to join them in a week or so but meanwhile my main problem was how to get back to Aden; since the Italians had come into the war it was more than ever difficult to get a passage. As soon as I could I went to the British Embassy and began plaguing Mr (now Sir Bernard) Burrows to help me find a ship. He promised to keep in touch and to let me know when he heard of a sailing, so I left Cairo by train with my baby for Heria. The nearest station to the village was Zagazig where Sheikh met us with a hired car.

Village life was just like being back in the Hadhramaut, for at that time a village in Egypt was as primitive as the most primitive of villages in Wadi Du'an. In Heria, famed as the birthplace of the great nationalist leader Arabi Pasha, there was no water supply, no electricity, no drainage, no medical facilities nearer than Zagazig, only a mosque school and the village *Omdah* to keep law and order. The Al Bar house was a mud bungalow with earth floors, oil lamps, and no modern sanitation, and I felt more at home in it than the family who continually bemoaned the luxuries of their Cairo flat. The villagers were very friendly and often invited us into their homes to take coffee with them, and the Imam of the mosque undertook to give Zahra her first Arabic lessons. Leila slept most of the day in a folding cot placed in a shady spot out of doors. It was a pastoral existence, with little to do but keep out of the sun, eat, sleep, play pat ball with tennis rackets on the hard baked earth, or walk round the village.

I was impatient to be back in Aden and felt it would be better to be on the spot in Cairo when news came of a ship. 'Papa' offered me the loan of the flat and so after just a week in Heria, Zahra, Leila and I moved back to Cairo where I tried to cope with running a home, greatly helped by Um Sabri who did all the shopping and cooking. There was no shortage of food in Egypt, although we seemed to live almost exclusively on a diet of pigeons, nor, except for one or two alarms, were there any serious air raids. But Mr Burrows still had no news for me and I threatened to remain in his office in his comfortable armchair until he found me a passage. At last I received word by telephone that we *might* get berths on a ship leaving from Suez the next day. I hired a car and set off with children and a mountain of luggage. I reported, as instructed, to the naval officer in charge who greeted me by handing me a signal he had just received: 'Mrs Ingrams is not repeat not to leave by S.S. –'. I presumed someone more important needed the cabin but 'there was a war on' and no one could explain. Back we had to trail to Cairo and fortunately, being of a pessimistic nature, I had kept the car waiting. A few days later I was advised to try again and this time we were more successful. Although I was glad to be going back to Aden I was sorry to be leaving Cairo; there is something about that lively, noisy and beautiful city which always draws me to return.

Chapter Thirteen

A VISIT TO YEMEN

Soon after Harold had taken up his post as Chief Secretary the Governor retired and when I returned from Egypt Harold was acting Governor. It was an anxious time with the evacuation of British Somaliland, frequent air raids by the Italians on Aden, though fortunately usually very ineffective, and continuing bad news from Europe. The following year however, Harold was back as Chief Secretary and able to get away from Aden to visit Yemen in order to discuss the never-ending controversy over the frontier between that country and the Aden Protectorate. It was an opportunity for us to visit a new country and we took the family with us, including Melahi, the lively Somali ayah whose tales of her childhood made one's hair stand on end. She could show you the scar on her neck where her father had stabbed her for refusing to marry the man chosen for her, and you felt the pain she and other Somali girls suffered as she described how they were sewn up so that they could not have intercourse with a man before marriage.

Salih Jaffer, the Political Agent of the British Government in Hodeida and brother-in-law of the Jaffer girls who had been my first Arab contacts in Aden, came too. Before leaving, he and I went to the bazaar to buy presents for the Imam, his sons and their wives. We called on one of the many Indian silk merchants where we sat drinking iced coffee while fingering rich silks, and finally chose a gold-embroidered coat length for the Imam with three white and gold turbans for his sons, and some brightly coloured finely woven veils for the women.

We set off by car for Taiz early one morning, crossing through part of the Western Aden Protectorate to the frontier with Yemen. It was a bumpy drive, mostly along dry river beds, and as Taiz is 4000 feet above sea level there was a lot of climbing and it took seven and a half hours to cover the 123 miles from Aden. The scenery became much greener as we neared Taiz, some men were grazing their goats, a thing one never saw in the Hadhramaut, where herding goats was women's work. It was dark when we drove up the hill into Taiz and saw the lights of the guest house ahead of us. The Taiz customs post that barred the road was raised for us and as we drove on we could see bunting strung between poles, not in our honour but in honour of the Governors of Hodeida and Ibb, Princes Abdulla and Hasan, sons of the Imam, who were visiting their elder brother the Crown Prince. Servants in long white shirts and black velvet waistcoats stood waiting at the door of the guest house with lanterns, and led the way upstairs to a sitting-room where several tables had been placed together, covered with a white cloth, ready for our supper. In the next room beds were arranged in rows like a dormitory and covered with mosquito nets. It was all very clean, and after enjoying a good meal we went straight to bed.

When I woke in the morning I was reminded of Switzerland; voices were sharp in the dry, crisp air and the sounds from the valley were made clearer by the altitude. Green hills encircled the town and from the northern windows of the guest house we looked down on white mosques, houses of brown mud decorated with whitewash, and gardens filled with trees. I was surprized that there was so much green in Taiz. We watched a continuous procession going to and from the Crown Prince's palace which lay farther up the hill. There were soldiers cantering along on horseback, men on mules, on donkeys, or on camels, but mostly on foot, often walking in pairs with linked hands. There was so much activity that we thought the people were paying their respects to the visiting governors, but Salih Jaffer said it was quite usual for crowds to go to the palace every day with complaints – they would have to pay their way into the royal presence or pay to have their petitions laid before the Crown Prince. Women in tight-fitting dark blue trousers, with their blue robes tucked up, passed by carrying firewood on their heads. The Chief Magistrate rode slowly down the hill under a cream umbrella held over his head by a soldier, while another carried his portfolio. Every now and again he was halted by petitioners who leaned forward to kiss his knee or the hem of his robe. It was all very medieval.

Though this was still Arabia it was not at all like the Hadhramaut. For one thing the Yemeni men wore long brown or white shirts with a belt of cartridges round their waists and a dagger thrust behind the buckle. Sometimes their heads were covered by skull caps, sometimes by casually wound turbans, into which most of them placed a sprig of some sweet-scented shrub. Then, though their features sometimes showed a mixture of Arab with Ethiopian or other African blood, they did not, as in the Hadhramaut, show any traces of East Indian blood. They might have been a far more prosperous community than the Hadhramis as they lived in a fertile country, but there was at that time no apparent desire to leave the Middle Ages for the twentieth century and benefit from the know-how of other countries. One reason for the apathy of the average Yemeni was, I am sure, due to their addiction to *qat* (*catha edulis*), the most debilitating, time-wasting scourge of Yemen. The leaves of the shrub are chewed to give the addict a feeling of being on top of the world, of being able to solve all problems, but the after effects are lassitude, apathy and depression. Every Yemeni who could afford it, and most of them got hold of *qat* somehow, spent the afternoons with his friends chewing, spitting, drinking water and chewing again. These sessions inspired a great deal of talk but no action and I saw no possibility of Yemen developing into a prosperous modern country so long as *qat* was allowed to exhaust the people's talents and sap their vitality.

We spent two quiet days in Taiz while Harold waited to see the Crown Prince, who was ill, writing, reading, listening to the news on the guest house wireless, and taking a walk through the main market street lined with shops selling cloth, grain, earthenware pots or general stores. We stopped to drink tea with the Syrian owner of a shop, a friend of Salih's, who was anxious to hear what Harold thought about the progress of the war. I found that it was ladies' day at the Turkish baths, a popular entertainment in Yemen inherited from the Turks who had ruled the country, on and off, for several hundred years. I was of course the only one who could go in, so leaving Harold and Salih with the Syrian, I walked along a passage and down a few steps into a circular room with three or four large niches and a fountain in the centre. Women and children sat on stone slabs in the niches stripped to the waist and wearing long cotton trousers in various colours. Some of them were drinking coffee and invited me to join them, but when I apologized and said I had no time a woman, whom I took to be the masseuse, as she looked businesslike and had a towel over her arm, took me by the hand to show me several smaller rooms with stone slabs, each one hotter than the other, and then into the steam room. The midday air seemed quite cool when I came out again into the street. On returning to lunch at the guest house we were glad to find that the cook had responded to our request for Yemeni food by giving us *khelba*, a purée of spinach with boiled meat, aubergine covered with sour milk, *bint as sahan* a cake-like pudding with honey, and goat's milk cheese eaten with barley bread.

From Taiz we drove to Mocha on the coast of the Red Sea, winding down the foothills to the Tihama, the coastal plain, where we were met by a hot wind that accompanied us the whole way to the sea. From a distance Mocha looked impressive with a lighthouse, tall white houses and clusters of palm trees, but on closer inspection it was but a sad ruin of past glories. When we walked through the streets we walked over mounds of what had once been brick houses, even the few remaining buildings were becoming covered by the sand. It was a sorry sight, for soon it seemed there would be no trace of this once renowned port with its European factories that had given its name to coffee. We stayed with the Governor of Mocha who had just been ordered by the Crown Prince (who was responsible for the district) not to leave Government House as he had been found out in some misdemeanour, but he was quite cheerful and Salih thought he would just be suspended for a while and then given a post elsewhere.

Government house was as dilapidated as the rest of Mocha, scantily supplied with carpets and a few wicker chairs. After a rather unpalatable meal we went early to bed, having to choose suffocation with the windows closed or letting in violent gusts of wind. Next morning we drove north along the beach where elegant pink flamingoes were looking for breakfast in the pools. The fishing villages of Yemen were unlike those on the south coast of Arabia for instead of rectangular or square huts made of sticks the people of the Tihama built round huts like those of Ethiopia. At Khokha where we stopped for lunch a guard of honour was waiting to salute Harold. This surprised us, but all Yemeni towns were linked by telegraph so that as soon as we left one town the next was informed of our expected time of arrival. During the afternoon a sandstorm raged round us causing the driver to lose the track several times, and it was so hot that he frequently had to stop the car to turn it into the wind and allow the engine to cool. Leila was then only ten months old and indifferent to her surroundings, content so long as she had food regularly and could sleep on someone's lap, but Zahra was nearly six and her bright eyes were alert to everything, though she could always fall asleep with the greatest ease at any moment, no matter how bumpy the road.

That night we stayed at the guest house in Beit al Faqih, or 'House of the Wise Man', a town renowned for learning. It was very hot so we slept on the roof-top, disturbed by the sentries in different parts of the town calling out to each other to make sure they were still awake, and at dawn by the most appalling din when the men said their prayers, each one shouting them aloud to show his neighbour that he was obeying the call from the minarets.

While Harold went to pay his respects to the Governor of Beit al Faqih, a little girl came in from next door to play with Zahra, and her elder sister, enveloped in her outdoor black cloak, asked me to visit their mother. Her guest room was most unusual; three of the walls were lined with two rows of couches, one above the other, both spread thickly with rugs. There were two shelves above them running the length of the walls entirely covered with an astonishing miscellany of objects: an ordinary coloured china bowl would have its base set into mud, more mud placed inside the bowl with an enamel plate set into it, then another bowl or jug set into mud on the rim of the plate, and balanced on top perhaps an aluminium spoon. One shelf had an imposing array of empty bottles of mineral water. My hostess probably had Ethiopian blood as she was taller than most Yemeni women, dark-skinned, with fuzzy hair kept in place by a yellow cotton handkerchief. Her sister-in-law was much fairer with a long curved nose and high cheekbones. They both wore tight fitting bodices of printed cotton with long sleeves and high necks, but the bodices barely met across their breasts, and there was an expanse of bare flesh between the bodices and their long skirts. I was sure that Fatima and her friends in Seiyun would have been shocked at this style of dress.

We travelled on across the coastal plain to the main port of Yemen, Hodeida, where the hot, enervating air was broken by a violent thunderstorm just as we arrived. This was the town where Salih Jaffer had his home and we were housed in the government guest house next door. The thunderstorm had done little to cool the air next day and we felt a distaste for doing anything very much. Harold had his beard trimmed by a local barber before calling on the Governor of Hodeida, and I exchanged news of Aden with Salih's wife, sister to Fakhria, Qadria and Rahima. The town had a sleepy air and there was little activity at the harbour, except for the sound of hammering where a new wharf was being built. Hodeida was mainly used by dhows carrying goods up and down the Red Sea or by the same ships that brought passengers and goods from Aden to Mukalla: it was rare at that time for a large ship to be seen in the port.

Leaving Hodeida we drove eastwards, escorted by a lorry full of soldiers, and climbed the foothills that were carpeted with gentians and thyme. The mountains ahead loomed up

Crowd watching us arrive at a town in Yemen (Ch. 13)

'Zahra and Leila were carried in wooden boxes slung on either side of a mule'
(Ch. 13)

Gleaner resting beside her baby's cradle

The stony wastes of the *jol*

formidably, their slopes covered with the terrace cultivation for which Yemen is famous, and the houses of the mountain villages standing out like pinnacles of rock. At sunset we stopped for the night at a village a hundred and six miles from Hodeida, outside a coffee shop owned by a kindly man with a hard-working wife and a simple-minded sister. The wife made us some excellent chicken soup and then the children, Melahi and I settled down in the car to sleep. Harold lay on a charpoy outside the shop, while Salih and the driver, who were both afraid of the cold, slept inside. When the sun came up we went for a walk in search of wild flowers while break-fast was being prepared, returning with good appetites for the freshly made millet bread which we dipped into sour milk.

During the morning we came to Hammam Ali (Ali's bath), a popular spa where the Imam sometimes came to bathe in the hot springs. It was a fashionable resort for the nobility but deserted at that time, except for the women's baths where several families were having a picnic. They had brought their charcoal cooking-stoves, their food, and their children, and many of the women were happily bathing naked in the enclosed pools where Melahi and I gossiped with them for a while.

In the afternoon we were brought to a standstill by a subsidence some thirty feet across and about six feet deep. One of the soldiers off the lorry went to the nearest village to get help as the villagers in Yemen were responsible for the upkeep of the roads, and if they did not maintain them properly soldiers were billeted on them until the work was done. When our soldier returned with some able-bodied men they were roughly rebuked for allowing the road to get into such a state. They rebuilt it quicker than I would have thought possible, but because of the delay we spent another night in the open. It was very cold on the mountainside but we were in a beautiful position looking over peaks and valleys which in the morning were shrouded with soft mist. As we continued climbing the scenery became even wilder, with towering jagged peaks on all sides. There were wild flowers everywhere, particularly beautiful were the tall white lilies,

I

and from the distant valleys we could hear the camel bells of passing caravans.

Quite suddenly we left the hills and came on to the stony plain on which stands the walled city of Sana, capital of Yemen. It was an anachronism to be driving in a motor-car up to the gate where only the previous day the heads of criminals had been displayed to show that Yemeni justice had been done. Two armed horsemen in long white shirts, caught at the waist by a belt of cartridges, were waiting to escort us to the guest house within the walls. It was a comfortable four-storeyed building with a garden and a tennis court, relic of some former foreign owner. The kitchen and servants' quarters were on the ground floor, occupied also by the soldiers who always followed us wherever we went, then came the sitting-room on the first floor furnished with tables and chairs, Salih's bedroom, a bathroom and a storeroom. Above that was our bedroom, the children's room and another bathroom, and the dining-room was at the top of the house.

At that time there were only a few Europeans in Sana, most of whom were concerned with the hospital, and our first visitors were the two doctors and the nurse from the Keith Falconer Mission in Aden. They were doing magnificent work in Sana in conditions which were by no means easy and often frustrating. Besides having their own clinic, Dr Petrie worked among the men at the hospital while Dr Croskery and Miss Cowie worked among the women patients. There were between two hundred and three hundred beds but they were short of all necessities and it was a perpetual struggle to get anything out of the government; all decisions rested finally with the Minister of Health, who was one of the royal princes. There was also an Italian doctor who literally divided the male patients with Dr Petrie, for the latter dealt with cases from the neck up while the Italian doctor dealt with them from the neck down. I never discovered who dealt with the patients' necks.

Sana was one of the most picturesque cities of Arabia, offering a living picture of medieval towns in Europe. I doubt if it has changed much since 1941 for Yemen is still far away from the twentieth century. There were streets of craftsmen, workers in iron, in copper, dagger-makers, tailors, shoemakers, gem polishers, and through these lanes wound a stream of men leading camels or riding donkeys, crying, 'Make way, make way'. Tribesmen from outlying districts, as well as the city dwellers, crowded round the grain shops where maize, wheat, barley, millet or other grain could be bought, piled high in locally woven sacks of black and white wool. The most crowded corner of all was where the *qat* leaves were sold, which must be bought as fresh as possible. I tried chewing *qat* and can only describe it as what I imagine it would be like to chew privet leaves.

In 1941 Sana still had its Jewish quarter, where Jews were free to practise their religion but were restricted in various other ways. They could not ride when a Muslim was walking, nor were they allowed to build houses of more than two storeys, although I went to the house of Habshas, a Jewish merchant, which was at least three storeys high. Another wealthy Jew, Yusuf Arabi, invited me to the wedding party of his daughter and she sat in a corner of the room wrapped in black clothes embroidered with gold. All the women guests wore black with scarves of black and red, and many of them stoically wore fur lined coats although the heat was terrific and perspiration poured down their faces. There was an orchestra consisting of two elderly women, one with a drum, the other with a brass tray on which there was a small ring, and when she tapped the tray underneath the ring danced about giving out a slight tinkling sound. It was not very exciting music but it seemed to be popular. Yusuf Arabi showed me photographs of female relations living in Palestine, looking very different from their Yemeni cousins, for they wore blouses and skirts, had their hair loose and wore no head-dresses. No doubt like the forty-two thousand other Jews from Yemen this family is now living in Palestine.

Imam Yahya, the king of the Yemen, was over seventy and was said to have at least forty children, but his queen, known to everyone as Sitt Fatima, was his one remaining wife and the mother of three princes and one princess. I met her when she invited me to tea at the palace, a modest building not much larger than many other Sana houses, and the women's quarters looked out on to an enclosed garden. The queen was much younger than her husband, a charming woman with natural dignity and a friendly manner, and she looked very elegant in a blue and white velvet dress with a blue and gold veil. We sat side by side on a mattress covered with Persian carpets, cushions at our backs, and tea, biscuits and tinned fruit was brought in on brass trays by servants who then sat round the wall joining in the conversation, which was mostly about our journey, the children, and what the Hadhramaut was like and how it compared to Yemen. After tea we walked in the garden with other members of the household who, in their long dresses with veils wound round their heads and kept in place by a wide kerchief, reminded me of pictures I had seen somewhere of court ladies in a Tudor garden.

The family of Raghib Bey, the Foreign Minister, became very friendly and we frequently went to his house. His wife was a vivacious, elderly Turkish woman and, having no children of her own, she had adopted several but she was worried by the lack of good schools in Sana. Her husband had recently taken a second wife, a nice fat jolly girl who had been a servant in the house. The senior wife assured me she was not at all jealous, in fact she had chosen the young woman for him as being suitable to look after him in his old age.

Ever since I had seen the Turkish baths in Taiz I was longing to try one and in Sana they were very popular, owing to the cold climate, and well-to-do people installed them in their houses. I was invited to take a bath in the house of Sheikh Ali Hamdani whose wife and daughter bathed with me. The baths were in the basement and we took off our clothes in an anteroom, wound a cloth round our waists and sampled in turn the three hot rooms, sitting on stone slabs talking through the misty vapour that rose through openings in the stone floors. When the bath attendant thought I was sufficiently cooked she came for me, laid me on a slab, poured hot water over me, washed my hair, scrubbed me all over with a glove, soaped me, washed me down again, and then wrapped me in towels and laid me out on a carpeted couch to dry.

During the six weeks we were in Sana Harold was having discussions with the Imam or his Foreign Minister about the frontier problems and matters connected with the tribes on either side of the frontier, and I was often kept busy coding and decoding telegrams to and from Aden. Harold also gathered a great deal of information on local Yemeni politics and on the attitude of Yemenis to the war, some of whom professed to be pro-Allies and some pro-Axis. It was difficult to believe there was a war in Sana; there were no food shortages, except for some imported goods such as rice, no air raids, and nothing to bring war close to us except listening to the news on the wireless. There was, however, a great deal of interest in the rebellion that broke out in Iraq, especially as there was a military mission from that country helping to train the Yemeni army. The mission remained sitting on the fence, unwilling to show which way their sympathies lay, until it was seen if Rashid Ali or the legitimate government won the day.

We left Sana, as we had entered it, escorted by horsemen who cantered alongside the car for several miles. The first night of our homeward journey was spent at Yerim, a dirty town with narrow lanes of muck made worse by a heavy downpour. It was picturesquely situated on a mountain with wonderful views but our night was made so hideous by fleas that we were in no mood to stay on to admire the view in the morning. Soon after leaving Yerim the motor track came to an end and we transferred ourselves and our belongings on to six mules and two donkeys. The only motorable track to Sana had been the one we had taken from Hodeida and as we wanted to see more of Yemen we chose to take the mountain road back to Taiz which could only be done by horse, mule or donkey. The fact that we had a small baby and a child with us was no deterrent for they could be carried in wooden boxes slung on either side of a mule. As Leila was lighter than Zahra she had to be weighed down with suitcases, but she was quite unperturbed and as the mule plodded on she slept most of the time, while Zahra sat up in her box, keeping up a running chatter with the muleteer.

We had to climb Jebel Sumara, 10,000 feet above sea level, by a narrow path that wound among the boulders and the terraces of green corn that crossed the mountain like giant steps. Villages were scattered up the slopes to the very summit, the houses perched as though a gust of wind would blow them away. There were wild flowers in full bloom on either side of the path, lilies, bluebells, yellow daisies, and many I did not know. Near the top of the mountain a fort built by the Turks was pointed out to us as marking the boundary between the Zeidis and Shafa'is, the two sects of Islam that divide Yemen into those (the Zeidis) whose spiritual as well as temporal head was the Imam, and those (the Shafa'is) who did not recognize the Imam's spiritual authority. It was this sectarian bitterness together with dissatisfaction at Imamic rule which led to revolution in September 1962.

Having reached the summit of Jebel Sumara, we had to make our way down the other side, by another narrow path on which the mule was often held up as the muleteer edged him slowly round rocks without damaging the boxes carrying Zahra and Leila. Reaching level ground, we stopped by a river where a short while before five men had been carried away by flood waters, but now it was peaceful among the mango trees, apricots, and bananas that lined the banks. By dusk we could see our night's resting place, Makhadar, a walled village on a mountain spur, and as we climbed the wide path leading to it we heard bugles and the voices of boys calling the people to prayer. A guard of honour of ten men lined the roadside, presented arms to Harold and fell in behind our procession. As we drew near the governor's castle one of them sounded a bugle. By now it was dark and lanterns shone from the windows like beacons welcoming us, and when we came up to the gate followed by the wild looking soldiers I thought of Duncan and his retinue approaching

Macbeth's castle, but hoped we would be more fortunate in our reception.

The medieval atmosphere of the night did not disappear in the morning as we watched the women bearing pots on their heads bringing water from the well outside the town, and oxen being led off to plough the fields with a donkey carrying their plough for them. Curiously many of the roofs in Makhadar had grass growing on them: they were built of earth and no doubt the grass seed sprang to life in the rainy season, but I did wonder who did the mowing.

It was May and spring flowers were all round us as we rode on to Ibb along lanes lined with mimosa, its scent filling the air. In Sahul the Saturday market was in full swing and the fresh fruit, the bright red earthenware pots, the vegetables and the babel of voices made a cheerful, colourful scene. Our little procession was an added attraction and we were quickly surrounded by men and women curious to see what was in the wooden boxes borne by the mule. Many of them had not seen a European child before and were amazed at Leila's fairness. As Ibb was not far away some of them attached themselves to us and when we approached the walled town, which, like Makhadar, is perched on a spur of a hill, we could see crowds lining the roof tops and every other vantage point. The stone houses were built so close together that the sunlight could hardly penetrate between them, and many of the windows still had the traditional alabaster which gives a soft dim light to the rooms whilst keeping out the cold but glass was increasingly replacing alabaster in Yemeni towns and though less picturesque it was more practical. The house which the Governor of Ibb had put at our disposal was on the edge of the town and had an uninterrupted view of the green valley. In the morning we had a quick look at the town, which, strangely enough, reminded me of St Malo in Brittany, perhaps because of its high, well-built walls and the main square where food was offered for sale from stalls set under the branches of a large tree, but in place of the parish church there was a mosque with a tapering minaret.

As usual we set off before breakfast, stopping after an hour or so to eat the food always provided by our hosts for both breakfast and lunch, flat slabs of bread, hard-boiled eggs, cold chicken, cucumber, bananas and mangoes, or even plums and apples, for Yemen with its varied altitude and climate produced almost any kind of fruit and vegetable. Between Ibb and Taiz there was another mountain, Jebel Mahmul, and we laboriously climbed for several hours, pausing only a short while at the top before descending the other side. This was a tricky descent as the mules slithered on the rocky paths still wet with recent rain. Once on flat ground we had not far to go before reaching the village where a car and a lorry sent by the Crown Prince were waiting for us. Rain came down in torrents as we drove for three hours to Taiz, thinking ourselves lucky to be in the shelter of a car.

Chapter Fourteen

MUKALLA AGAIN

After nearly two years in Aden we were to return to the Hadhramaut where Harold felt his real work lay and where there was still much to be done. The war was now having its effect on South Arabia as it was no longer concentrated in Europe; the battle for British Somaliland, its loss to the Italians and its recapture, the liberation of Ethiopia, the war in North Africa, had all brought more and more local participation. Then, when the Japanese overran the East Indies, the remittances on which their lives depended no longer arrived and the war was really brought home to the Hadhramis.

I was sorry in many ways to be leaving Aden, although the 'streamed' life there was much less attractive than the informal intermingling of everyone in the Hadhramaut. The 'A Stream', represented by the British community, was one in which I was never completely at ease, with the exception of a few kindred nonconformists, the 'B Stream' of notable Arab families, Parsees, and other non-British Top People, was where I found many congenial friends, and the 'C Stream' or 'the rest' was the most interesting, varied and attractive for finding both friends and congenial companions. It always seemed strange to me that so many British women could live for years in Aden without ever speaking to an Arab other than their servants or the shopkeepers. They had no interest in the 'natives', did not attempt to speak a word of Arabic, and were astonished if a compatriot did not conform to their way of life – bridge, tea parties, the exclusive British club. This was not true of missionaries, nor of wives of political officers who were often as immersed in local Arab life as their husbands, but it was true of many Service wives and a good many mercantile families, not only British but French, Italian or Greek, and certainly there was only a handful of foreign women who ever went into an Arab home. Yet in

Aden the Arab women were often more educated than those in the Hadhramaut. There was a flourishing girls' elementary school, a secondary school was starting, and there was a convent school to which a number of Arab families sent their daughters. In spite of this only one or two brave souls ventured out of doors without a veil, and even they dared not shed the all-enveloping black cloak. The most emancipated women were those in the Hasanali family, cousins of the Jaffers and, like them, of Persian origin. One of them in particular, Nebia, a forthright young woman with a mind of her own, pioneered Arab women's participation in social work. She joined various welfare committees and together with Rahima Jaffer and her sisters helped me to get together sewing parties to make bandages. It is true, Nebia was something of a social climber and liked to be mixing with 'the Best People', and for this she was later to come under fire from more nationalist-minded women, but in 1941, when Arab women represented nearly half the entire population, Nebia drew attention to that hidden, potentially powerful but secluded section by mingling socially with European women, who, if they thought about Arab women at all, thought of them as the wives of their servants.

The British Council opened a club for women in Aden, in the hope of bringing them into more active participation in the community, but it was uphill work as few men would allow their womenfolk such emancipation as joining a club, and it was largely patronised by Indians, Somalis, a few Europeans, and by the Hasanali-Jaffer families. The strictly purdah bandage-making parties, however, were successful in attracting a number of the more secluded women especially as they were thought to be working in a good cause. I had prepared the ground by talking for hours to the heads of the families, who in many cases needed personal persuasion, but I have no doubt that I was helped by the fact that Harold was the Chief Secretary. We had a good time at the working parties with, of course, tea and *sambusa* – cakes of wafer-thin pastry. When we had filled the first half dozen cases with bandages I asked the president of the Red Cross to accept them. Not for the first time I was amazed at the tactless and patronising way in which a European spoke to Arab women. She looked at the first case and said, 'The bandages all look very neat on top, perhaps I'd better look underneath to see if they're all like that.' It may have been intended as a joke but Arab women are as aware as anyone else when they are being treated like children and naturally resent it. *Kibr ingliz*, 'English pride', was an expression often used by Arabs and frequently deserved.

In fairness to the Englishwomen in Aden it must be admitted that it was not easy to make friends with Arab women who spoke no English and who never joined their husbands when there were Anglo-Arab parties. Arabic is a difficult language to learn and those who tried to master it usually got discouraged very quickly; in any case there was little incentive to persevere in Aden as there were so many other distractions besides drinking tea in an Arab home, but this lack of contact gave most European women the false impression that Arab women were unsophisticated, even childish, with little knowledge of the world around them. This was by no means true in Aden where I found my friends had a great deal to say about local affairs as well as about the war, but they did not at that time actively participate in politics – this was to come a few years later – but the bandage-making parties were in some measure a prelude to the emancipation which Aden women enjoy today.

Returning to the Hadhramaut meant leaving friends in Aden, but one of them was to come with us, Rahima Jaffer, the adventurous sister of the Jaffer family. I was anxious to encourage the Mukalla women to take part in outside activities, perhaps by getting them also to make bandages for the war effort, or perhaps by starting some sort of club, or even adult education, and for all this it was going to be invaluable to have Rahima's help. She was a Muslim and could show that it was not only Christians who took part in interests outside the home. It was the first time she had ever left her family, and when I went round to pick her up I found all her relations had gathered to say goodbye.

Rosewater was poured on to our hands and incense was wafted in front of us as we walked to the front door where Rahima's mother stood with the Quran in her hand to hold it over our heads in blessing as we left.

Back once again at the Residency in Mukalla we felt after a few days as if we had never been away. Melahi, the ayah, did not want to leave the flesh-pots of Aden so we had engaged a local Somali, Ifteen, to look after Zahra and Leila. Zahra had started school in Aden and in Mukalla she learned Arabic with Sheikh Abdulla, a school-teacher who later became Director of Education, while for her general education I struggled to follow the syllabus of the P.N.E.U. (Parents National Education Union). This was a wonderful method for mothers with no idea of teaching as all the lessons were set out most clearly and examination papers were sent from England to make sure the child was keeping up to standard. Unfortunately for Zahra I was not as well organised as the P.N.E.U. and being pre-occupied with office work I would often leave her for an hour or more on a lesson which was supposed not to last more than twenty minutes.

Rahima's education had ended when she was eight and although she could recite passages from the Quran she had but scant knowledge of anything else, so she joined in Zahra's history and geography lessons and very quickly became fluent in English. I also became involved in teaching the reading of Arabic to primary schoolchildren. A girls' school had been started in Mukalla about a year before we returned, due to the enterprise of Sheikh Abdulla who persuaded a number of parents to send their daughters to be taught by his wife and daughter. He was a much respected man so he soon had quite a number of girls who were only allowed to remain at school until they went into purdah at the age of nine or ten. This small beginning expanded over the years into a number of primary schools and a large secondary school, but in 1942 Sheikh Abdulla and his family were still carrying on the struggle against prejudice. He had the encouragement of Harold's Educational Assistant, Sheikh Qaddal, a remarkable and inspiring teacher from Sudan. He was running teacher training courses but because of purdah Sheikh Abdulla's wife and daughter could not attend them and I was asked to take the course and then pass on what I learned to the two women teachers. Thus I came to give demonstration lessons on teaching kindergarten children to read Arabic, not entirely successfully as when I tried to explain how a certain Arabic letter should be written by showing the picture of a camel, I forgot that a camel has at least a hundred different names in Arabic and not one of the forty children called out the name I needed to explain the letter on the picture.

Sheikh Abdulla may have been progressive in education but he was a traditionalist in his own home. When his wife, Fatima, did not produce a son he decided to take a second wife. Fatima was very depressed, for which she was scolded by her friends who thought it natural that Sheikh Abdulla should want a son, and when he married Safiya, a younger woman, Fatima left the house in a fury and he had to cajole her to return home. I went to the party given to cement the reunion of the family and the two wives sat side by side in silence while their guests cheerfully chatted to each other. Servants brought in two identical boxes, placing one in front of each wife, and opening them they found identical presents, a dress, a veil, scent, and a cake of soap. Fatima gave a faint smile but scarcely looked at her presents.

Rahima helped me to arrange regular sessions for bandage-making by first going round to different houses and talking to the wives of some of the prominent men of Mukalla, telling them how useful they could be, how it would give them an enjoyable afternoon out, and how, as important people, they should set an example to others. Our efforts were given royal patronage, which was a great help, when the Sultana in the old palace offered us a large room there for the meetings and, as nowhere could be more respectable, it made it easier to persuade husbands to allow their wives to join the weekly meetings. We worked hard and sent off large quantities of bandages made from bales of cloth given by local merchants, but we also enjoyed a good deal of light-hearted gossip about the latest marriages or divorces, and sometimes more serious talk on such matters as the differences between Islam and Christianity, particularly in relation to women. The meetings ended with tea and cakes, occasionally with drumming and singing, but as soon as we saw the sun setting in the sea the women rose to leave, picking up their identical black cloaks from the floor, sniffing them to recognize their own scent, then, wrapping themselves from head to foot with a veil over their faces, they slipped into their sandals and quietly set off down the five flights of stairs to the side door, hushing anyone whose voice rose above a whisper as it was not seemly to let men hear you speaking.

As it seemed clear that the women enjoyed getting together in this way I asked one or two of them their reactions to the idea of opening a 'room for women', we dared not call it a club or none of them would have been allowed to come. They were enthusiastic and with their advice and help we rented a room with a courtyard and a kitchen where we could make tea, play games, look at the pictures in the magazines, or just talk. Rahima, by request, gave sewing and reading lessons, we also did physical exercises which were quite hilarious but which we hoped were keeping us slim. We discussed hygiene, the care of children, the menace of flies, anything at all that was of interest, but we never talked long on any serious subject or it became boring. I learned a great deal about their commonsense attitude towards the upbringing of children and found that we shared many of the 'old wives' tales' on how to cure various ailments. They began to understand cause and effect, that mosquito larvae in an earthenware water pot can bring fever, or that flies bring dirt, and when their interest was aroused by something they saw in a magazine I would do my best to explain anything they did not understand. I never wanted to thrust advice down their throats as it has always seemed to me a gross impertinence to go into someone else's house and tell them how to run it.

We had not long been back in Mukalla when Rahima and I went off on a short excursion by donkey. Salih Ali, who had so often been on trips with us, was the instigator of this one. He had been told by some beduin that a most unusual object like the mummified body of a human or an animal lay in a shallow cave half way up a steep cliff, impossible to reach except by a rope from the top of the cliff. Our curiosity was aroused but when we arrived at the spot after two days' ride, the object, seen through binoculars, appeared to be just a piece of wood. However having come so far we thought we might as well make sure what it was. One of the beduin, Muhammad Ali, volunteered to be lowered down the perpendicular cliff for a closer look, but first insisted that I should give him a note to the Jinn of the cliff not to harm him. In all solemnity I wrote on a piece of paper: 'To the Jinn of the cliff. I request you to allow Muhammad Ali to pass freely without let or hindrance,' signed it and gave it to Muhammad who tucked it confidently into his belt. The Jinn proved to be friendly and Muhammad returned with a six-foot, irregular shaped piece of wood that had notches carved on it by some byegone hand. That was all. But in spite of the disappointing result the trip made an enjoyable break from the Mukalla routine.

Harold and I often made journeys up country by car, sometimes taking Rahima and the children with us. It was now possible to reach Wadi Hadhramaut by car either via Shihr and Tarim or through Du'an to Shibam. The steep passes from the plateaux to the valleys that had been cut for motor-cars were an astonishing achievement. They had the most hair-raising hairpin bends and the gradients seemed almost perpendicular. Lorries were already being imported in considerable numbers and were negotiating these passes with some difficulty, though usually in safety. At times the beduin held up the traffic, afraid that their livelihood was being threatened, but Harold advised on legislation giving them security by preventing too many lorries taking over the transport of goods; and it was not many years before young beduin learned to drive and became lorry-drivers themselves.

When I revisited the Hadhramaut by air in 1963 our journeys by camel or donkey, even the early car journeys, seemed to belong to another age, as distant from today as the wagon trains of the American west, but I was glad that I had

had the chance of seeing the Hadhramaut from the back of a camel for otherwise I would never have got to know the country or the people so well. Unfortunately the Hadhramaut, like the rest of South Arabia, jumped almost straight from camel to air travel because roads were never fully developed; although air travel may create pockets of development it can never have the same all-over developing effect as a network of good roads.

Chapter Fifteen

CAMEL PATROL

The development in the Hadhramaut that took place after 1937, the medical services which had cost £350 a year in 1934 and £5,000 ten years later, the educational services that rose from £450 a year to £11,000, agricultural developments and improved administration, none of this could have happened unless there had been peace, and peace would not have been maintained without the formation of the Hadhrami Beduin Legion. Harold set up this force in 1938, bringing together tribesmen from different tribes to serve in policing the country, in spreading education, in giving medical help, arbitrating, and developing a sense of trust between the various sections of the community. In the early stages of recruitment there was some suspicion as to why the force was being formed but it was not long before tribesmen were enlisting from all over the country. The motive may often have been the prospect of good pay and good food but the Legionary soon found he was learning to accept erstwhile enemies as friends and appreciating the benefits of order and justice. The Legion had its headquarters near Mukalla and also had two forts in widely separated parts of the country. These forts were bases from which the Legionaries operated in desert and nomadic areas and as they were built near a well, the focal point for all local tribesmen, the Legionaries soon became as important a part of the lives of the tribesmen as the well itself, especially as they not only arbitrated in disputes but some Legionaries were trained to run a first aid post, and others to give first lessons in reading, writing and arithmetic to beduin children.

There were large areas of the country where the work of the Legion was unknown, as relief forces for the garrisons at the forts were taken to them by lorry from Mukalla along the main roads. Harold decided that a regular camel patrol

K

of Legionaries from headquarters should relieve the garrisons by using cross-country camel tracks, thus making contact with distant tribes. Muhammad Ba Matraf, the interpreter who shared the burden of censoring letters with me, was to accompany the patrol in order to pay the salaries of the Legionaries at the forts and to see if there were any problems, and Harold suggested that I might also like to go. Our instructions were to set up nightly halts at regular intervals for use by future patrols, make contact with as many tribes as we could, pay the garrisons, and report on our activities.

The Hadhrami Beduin Legion camels were strong riding camels which could cover the ground very fast but as this was to be a journey of over five hundred miles our orders were to travel slowly, resting the camels for ten minutes every hour. This was no doubt good for the camels and it was not long before I thought it was also good for me. We carried a tent, similar to those used in Jordan (Transjordan then) and, except when we stayed at the forts, it was our home for a month. We were well organised. Each man knew his sleeping place in the tent and exactly where to put his saddle and his belongings. Two would fetch firewood, another two would do the cooking, and there was always one on guard. When supper was ready we sat in a circle round the large dish and ate with our fingers from the rice in front of us until the last grain was gone. After drinking tea I moved my things outside and settled down to sleep. The lanterns went out soon after eight o'clock and then there was silence but for human and camel snores, or the sentry waking Sergeant Umar to ask him the time.

Travelling with soldiers, even though under the uniforms they were still beduin at heart, was very different from travelling with easy going seiyids. We were woken each morning by Sergeant Umar's whistle at four o'clock, when it was still dark. Astir at once, coffee was prepared, the tent taken down, and the camels saddled. After a cup of beduin coffee (ginger-flavoured) and a handful of dates we took up positions by the couched camels. At the command '*Num*' (sleep), the camels put their heads to the ground and we all mounted. They remained motionless until the order '*Qum*' (get up), when they rose in their ungainly fashion and we were off. We rode in the same formation every day, Salmin the Stutterer in front, followed by Zeid from Hajr and Ba Dhams from Libna, then came Muhammad Ba Matraf and myself, Sergeant Umar, Ahmed Bursheid of Libna, Salim the Akbari, and at the back the youngest member of the patrol, Salmin Tanbuli. He was our mascot, a delightful lad of about fifteen with long curly hair and a friendly grin. Each night Muhammad and I dug holes and put up a notice board as a sign to future patrols where their night's halt should be. Beduin soon appeared to see what we were doing and we invited them into the tent to share a cup of coffee, when we were able to tell them about the Legion and its work. If they were surprised at first at seeing a woman with the patrol they accepted it as natural when they heard I was 'Ingrams' woman', who was known to travel round the countryside.

After climbing the coastal hills to the plateau, some 5,000 feet above sea level, we rode eastwards towards Leijun, one of the Legion's forts. On the third day we came to Reidat al Ma'ara, the most populous area on the route. Here we found that all but one of the water holes were dry and the people preparing to leave in search of grazing in the valleys. There had been an unusually long drought everywhere and this, added to the restrictions on remittances and on the import of food, was bringing great hardship. Among the men and children who gathered round us I noticed a blind boy with a swollen stomach and matchstick legs. He was covered with sores and it was obvious that left in his present condition he would not survive. I asked his uncle if he would take the boy by donkey to Mukalla where he would be looked after, and on his promising to do so I gave him a note for Harold: 'Here is one blind child. Please look after him and give bearer two rupees.' I went on not knowing whether he would ever reach Mukalla, but he did and he became the first pupil in a school that Harold started for handicapped children.

We set up five camping sites on the plateau, and on the

sixth day we saw the whitewashed towers of Leijun fort on the horizon. We were all glad as it meant a rest for two days, and Salim the Akbari had a stomach upset. At the lunch halt he had insisted that he wanted to be branded on the soles of his feet to take away the pain, but Salmin the Stutterer believed in herbal remedies and cooked the leaves of a plant that grew with determination among the stones and gave Salim the water to drink. It had the desired effect and we continued riding towards Leijun over the flat, stony plateau with scarcely a shrub to break the monotony. It was so monotonous that I read an *Argosy* Magazine to pass the time as I rode along on my camel. It was dark as we drew near the fort and heard soldiers trotting towards us singing, 'Oh Leijun, welcome to the sons of the tigers. Leijun which is surrounded by barbed wire and full of ammunition made by the Christians.'

Leijun was a romantic Beau Geste-type fort and we sat eating supper by the light of lanterns with equally romantic looking Legionaries. One of them set up my bed on the parapet and in the morning I woke to the sound of drilling. Some of the men were on parade, others were drawing water from the well in the courtyard, whilst others were kneading dough to make bread for breakfast. Muhammad and I held a kit inspection during the morning, combining it with a pay parade. This caused a lot of argument as there were a number of discrepancies between what we thought they should have and what the Legionaries expected to get. It took us a whole morning to sort it out but after that we could relax, wash our clothes and enjoy the comfort of feeling clean again.

On the second day we set out with a new batch of Legionaries but still with Sergeant Umar in command. As we rode away we sang our farewell: 'I give you a thousand salaams, oh white tipped fort, the resort of tigers.' We were now making for the other fort at Bir Asakir in the far north west, travelling by a cross-country route over the plateaux to Qa'udha in Wadi Hadhramaut, then along the wadi in a westerly direction. For several days we rode across the plateaux, passing many deserted settlements with dried up water holes. It was difficult to buy fodder but in one village there was still some green and we stopped by the only hut where there was a sign of life. An old man came out with his two sons; the other inhabitants, they told us, had gone off to seek grazing elsewhere. They had a store of fodder so we bought eighteen sheaves for a Maria Theresa dollar (about two shillings) and when the old father shook my hand as we left I saw that he had neither fingers nor toes. His son followed us to ask if we had any medicine for leprosy.

At every meal beduin appeared from nowhere to share the food, bemoaning the lack of rain which was driving them from their homes. At the large tribal settlement of Sah the headman looked gaunt and worried. He told us that they were more fortunate than others because they had springs, but they too were suffering from the drought. It was a pretty place, refreshing to look at with its many palm trees and bright green millet, a change from the parched up areas we had seen on our way. Many tribesmen from Sah emigrated to East Africa but in spite of this none of those who came to see the patrol had ever seen anything like me before. One man was so suspicious of a Christian that he thought the tea I offered him might have wine in it. The headman asked me about our English sultan and was surprised when Muhammad Ba Matraf could give a personal account of him and his home – he had been to Buckingham Palace as an interpreter at King George VI's coronation. We were told that only a few days previously the Sei'ar tribe, known as the wolves of Arabia, had raided two caravans taking camels and money.

We rode on from Sah among yellow flowering bushes and birds singing in the branches of the thorny *'elb* trees, but by the following day Sah's underground water must have come to an end for there was then the most desolate plateau I had yet seen. It stretched flat and empty for mile upon mile with neither bush nor plant, nothing but brown stones, and the only sign of life, apart from ourselves, was a lizard scurrying out of reach of the camels' feet. To relieve the monotony I recited the part of Juliet, maddened by the lines I had forgotten since the years it had been so familiar to me, when I was acting in Ireland with Anew McMaster's Shakespearian company. Then, as though growing out of the stones, we suddenly came across two forts with stone hovels nestling round them. Here we stopped for the night, but no one came to share our meal, the village was completely deserted.

On the fifth day after leaving Leijun we could see the distant cliffs of Wadi Hadhramaut and descended by a gradual pass to Qa'udha, situated in one of the widest parts of the wadi, which looked to us extremely civilized with its conglomeration of large whitewashed houses. Hakm Mbarek, the cheerful chieftain of the Nahdi tribe which centres round Qa'udha, invited us to lunch which we shared with ten pilgrims on their way to Mecca. They spoke no language anyone could understand and apparently had walked all the way from India.

None of the Legionaries knew the way to Bir Asakir from Qa'udha so we took on a guide, an apostle-like man with long hair, good features and a beard, called Ahmed Lakharash. He was dressed like all the northern beduin in a long off-white shirt, and his camel was smartly turned out with tasselled saddle cover and brilliantly coloured woollen saddlebags. My camp-bed was on the point of collapse but as we were now travelling over sand I slept on the ground, usually at a short distance from the tent and within sight of the sentry who paced back and forward throughout the night. Since leaving Leijun one of the Legionaries, Abdulla, had taken charge of me, fussing over me like an ayah when I went to bed, seeing that I had all I wanted. In the morning he woke us all with his chant, 'Who wants to sleep let him sleep but the father of Ahmed (meaning himself) never sleeps.' He brought me coffee as the first light shone on the wadi walls and we set off by five o'clock, not silently stealing away nor quietly folding our tent for it invariably crashed down with a resounding thud. As we rode away the hills would gradually light up in gold and rose, then the sky turned from a deep to a light blue, always cloudless and heralding the coming heat. This cool lovely time of day was all too short for in an hour or so the sun glared down, turning the landscape from its gentle smooth outline into harsh burning rocks and sand.

The first day or so after leaving Qa'udha we rode among fields of wheat, as since the peace many new wells had been dug. Then, as the wadi widened, there was only sand, hard and firm where the caravans had been passing for centuries, but away from the track the dunes rose and fell in endless procession. There was no shade and we had long tiring rides between the scattered wells, all bearing the names of women though no one could tell me why. We met caravans bringing grain from Yemen, some of them with stories of being raided by the Sei'ar tribe. Our meals were frugal and our routine rigorous and I found that when one is deprived of normal comforts, food, or other amenities, these wants are satisfied in dreams. Almost every night I dreamed I was in London, buying clothes, eating at restaurants, going to the theatre, or doing something a thousand times removed from the Hadhramaut desert.

The day we reached Bir Asakir was the longest ride of all. We not only had the searing heat of the sun but we had to battle against a furious sandstorm. All our discomforts were forgotten, however, when we had bathed, fed well and rested in the fort that was even more romantic than Leijun as it was surrounded by a desert of sand.

The commanding officer had made himself so popular that he had been given a local girl to marry for whom he had paid 227 Maria Theresa dollars, about £20, which was considered to be a lot of money – but then she was very pretty. There had been many recruits from the surrounding tribes and their women camped in goat-hair tents near the fort. They washed and cooked for their husbands, and I spent much of my time watching one grinding corn, singing to herself as her body swayed backwards and forwards over the grindstone, or another suckling her ten day old baby, born outside the tent with less fuss than a camel would have made. The father of one family had been posted to Mukalla and his wife asked me to tell him to send her some saucepans. A little girl sat nursing a baby who had diarrhoea and wiped up the mess with straw in a most unconcerned way. On the whole the children looked well on their diet of millet bread and goat's milk, so did their mothers who appeared much healthier than their sisters in the towns.

I bought a sheep to give the Legionaries for their dinner and watched the method they used to give everyone a fair share. After it was cooked the mutton was cut up into a sufficient number of pieces for each man to have one, then a soldier sat outside where he could not see the meat and another put his hand on a portion and called to the man outside 'For whom?' The man outside shouted the name of one of the soldiers who received that portion, so it went on until all the meat had been given out.

The third and last lap back to Mukalla was the longest and no European had yet visited most of the country. We had to retrace our steps along Wadi Hadhramaut to the mouth of Wadi Rakhia where we turned south to follow its course. Our first lunch halt was at the village of Amqan where we found a splendid spreading *'elb* tree to give us some shade. These trees, (*Zizyphus Spina Christi*) are of great importance to the economy. The trunks are used in building, the leaves eaten by camels and goats, and the fruit, a hard green berry, is dried and pounded into a paste. In times of drought it was often the only food available.

The headman of Amqan fetched water for us and a woman volunteered to get firewood. Another took one look at my sunburnt arms and brought henna to cool them. Each man tried to make us go to his home for coffee, but instead we served them from our pot under the tree. I gave out aspirin and epsom salts and put drops into the eyes of one child after another, but alas many of them were beyond hope, their sight lost through unintentional neglect.

It was a different story at the village of Tereif for there the women fled to safety when they saw us, not knowing what was in store for them. The men ventured out of their houses and filled one of our water skins, refusing to fill any more as they said their well was so deep it was difficult to bring the water to the surface, but we thought they were probably afraid of their well drying up – and who could blame them for being careful?

Whenever we passed through a tribal settlement we also passed the graveyard and I noticed what a large proportion of graves were those of children. For some years I had been enquiring about the number of children who died in infancy, and from the statistics I had gathered had come to the conclusion that about 75 per cent of children born alive died before they were two years old. This seemed an enormous percentage, but when one remembers the hardships, the ignorance, the lack of medical attention, this high proportion was not surprising.

The pass from Wadi Rakhia up to the plateau was one of the most difficult I had ever climbed and as camels are not as surefooted as donkeys on stony ground we walked, setting off from the wadi at dawn. All was quiet but for the crying of unseen monkeys. The air was intoxicating and although the path was steep I felt as if I had wings on my feet. I was well ahead of the rest of the patrol and when after two hours I reached the top I surprised a beduin who was just beginning the descent. 'Where have you come from?' he asked in astonishment. 'From the wadi', I replied. He went on his way shaking his head none too sure he had not seen a Jinn. There was another beduin with a flock of sheep and on seeing me he withdrew to a safe distance. 'Where have you come from?' he shouted. Nothing would induce him to come near me until the patrol arrived when he recognized the sort of people he knew.

As we continued over the plateau we saw a solitary black figure coming towards us but when about two hundred yards away he stopped, calling out, 'Where are you from?' The Legionaries replied, 'From the north. Come over, we can't hear you because of the wind.' The man cried out something which sounded like 'Go back the way you have come.' Again the soldiers asked him to come nearer but in reply he fired at us. Immediately the soldiers couched their camels and mine, being well trained, followed suit. They raised their guns to fire but Sergeant Umar ordered them to wait. The man, perhaps thinking it was better to be safe than dead, disappeared from view.

We crossed Reidat ad Deiyin where I had travelled with Seiyid Hasan three years earlier and found that on the whole the extension to the truce had been well kept. I was now in familiar territory and in the Bursheid country met Awadh in whose house I had once spent a night. He told us that there had been trouble between tribes on the road ahead of us and that it might not be possible for Harold to meet me by car at Mola Matar as we had arranged. There was still some way to go before joining the motor road from Mukalla to Du'an and on the way we met several caravans and the beduin confirmed that parts of the motor road had been broken by the Akabira tribe. When we reached Mola Matar there was no sign of Harold but I knew he would get a message through to me if he could not come, so we waited, keeping a constant watch in case the rumours of trouble were true and the Akabira, whose territory was nearby, made an attack. It had taken twenty-nine days to cover 530 miles and our camels had suffered from lack of fodder. At the end of the journey I found that my camel's hump had quite disappeared; the process of using up this reserve of fat had been so gradual that I did not realise until then that instead of being perched high on a hump, my saddle was on a back almost as flat as that of a horse.

On the second day there was a cloud of dust on the horizon and Harold appeared in his car, unperturbed, having settled the dispute with the Akabira. We drove back to Mukalla with Muhammad Ba Matraf, the patrol arriving two days later.

Chapter Sixteen

FAMINE

Travelling with the Hadhrami Beduin Legion patrol, I had seen the beginning of what was to become a disastrous famine. It was caused by many factors – a long period of drought, the difficulty of importing grain in wartime, and the shortage of money with which to buy food when remittances from abroad came to an end, making the rich people poor, and the poor, unemployed. When I returned to Mukalla from the patrol measures were already in hand to try and combat the famine, the British Government had allocated money to set up food kitchens in Wadi Hadhramaut and to import and distribute grain. There was nothing anyone could do to make the rain fall but prayers for rain were offered up all over the country.

The blind boy I had sent to Harold was the first of a number of crippled and blind children who were brought to Mukalla when news got round that a school for them had been opened, and with the famine many children suffering from malnutrition were also brought by their parents. There were Huda and Ramadhan, so thin you could almost see through them; they were probably five or six years old but looked two or three and they had the faces of an old woman and an old man. Next came Hasan, a boy suffering from bronchitis as well as starvation, then there was Abuda whose legs were paralysed and whom Harold found desperately searching for scraps in a market-place; soon there were twenty-one children in the school. A Mukalla woman, a widow, looked after their food and clothing and a Somali woman came to teach them how to make mats and baskets. Later on the blind boys went to a blind merchant who taught them to read braille.

The food kitchens set up in Wadi Hadhramaut were too far away to be of use to the starving people living in other parts of the country, and news began coming in about the condition of women and children left in the villages to fend for themselves whilst the men went off to seek work. This was hard to find, as no one had any money to pay for labour, and some of the money allocated for famine relief went on road-building to give employment to the able-bodied men, but this did nothing to solve the problem of the women and children left at home. Lorries were constantly going from the coast to Wadi Hadhramaut with grain and returning empty and Harold let it be known that women and children could come in the lorries to Mukalla where they would be fed and looked after. At that time, 1944, there was only one hospital in Mukalla, and that was for men. It soon had to be extended into other houses to make room for the numerous old men who arrived half dead from starvation, but there was no-where to house the sick women and children who began arriving in the returning lorries. Rahima and I opened up part of an empty house and turned it into a makeshift hospital, with straw mats on the floor for beds and cotton coverlets bought in the bazaar. It was soon filled with emaciated women of all ages, some holding babies in their arms, while other children with enormous stomachs walked feebly on thin sticks of legs. Dr Ranade, the only doctor in Mukalla, came as often as he could to tell us what to do, but our first problem was to find helpers. No women in purdah would have been allowed to work there so I sought help amongst the able-bodied beduin women who arrived from up country. The most urgent necessity was to keep the patients clean. Rahima and I were constantly changing the pieces of cotton cloth filled with excreta or washing the bottoms of the sick, and though at first horrified at the idea of doing such lowly work the beduin 'nurses' we had taken on were soon following our example and became a team of willing helpers. I had never imagined that such frail bodies could house so many worms, some a foot long, and often vomited from the mouth, nor did I realize how starvation can bloat as well as emaciate. It was the children who were most pathetic, their enormous eyes gazed round in pitiful bewilderment, and they died so quietly, one moment I would be cradling a child in my arms helping him to sip water, the next his little head drooped and he was dead.

Ten days after opening the 'hospital' we had over eighty patients and I noted on the eleventh day that, 'although there are still fifteen to twenty deaths every day some of the sick seem to be definitely improving, which cheers one up tremendously'. It was a wonderful satisfaction and relief to see a child able at last to stand on his own feet when only a few days before he had been at the point of death, or to see the despairing eyes of the little girl whose mother had died of cerebral meningitis gradually become normal as she found security in the newly-opened beduin girls' school. In a famine there is so much human agony that it is possible to become almost inured to it, but there are pictures one can never forget, like the mother holding her dead baby to her dried up nipple, or the child that clung to her dead sister, the boy who lay for days in a coma, waking one morning to gaze at me with uncomprehending eyes and then dying without a sound.

Apart from the terrible physical condition of the women and children they were nearly all covered with lice and a delousing centre was fitted up to which the lorries came on arrival from up country. On some days more than a hundred women and children were brought there and we spent hours persuading those women who were fit enough to undress to go through the baths, where they were washed from head to foot, had their hair cut short, and were given clean clothes. The children enjoyed it but the adults had to be cajoled by the promise of food at the end. Those too weak to go through the delousing centre were sent straight to the hospital.

A school for beduin boys outside Mukalla had been opened some years before and with the famine it was soon filled to capacity by the addition of boys from famine areas who were still strong enough to take part in the normal school activities. Up to this time, however, there had been no school for beduin girls owing to the reluctance of parents to send their daughters to school, but hunger drives away prejudice and the opportunity was seized to start such a school as we knew the girls would be allowed to go where they were going to be fed and looked after. Sa'ad, the beduin mother of one of the children who had been in the hospital, was recruited to take charge of the school. She was intelligent, enthusiastic, firm but kind, and she soon had the little girls organized and saw to their cleanliness and their food. A master was loaned from the beduin boys' school to give them lessons in reading and writing, a man being able to do this as there was not the problem of purdah which prevented men teaching in the town girls' school. Rahima and I also did some teaching and played games with the girls, and she or I went every day to give out the rations of millet, rice, and dates. When I revisited Mukalla in 1963 the school was still there with Sa'ad as enthusiastic as ever. Nearly twenty years had passed since the first dozen frightened little girls had been reassured by Sa'ad's firm understanding; hundreds had since passed through her hands, some to return to their tribal settlements, some to marry in Mukalla, and a few to carry on as teachers or as nurses.

In addition to the beduin boys and girls schools which catered for tribesmen's children, something needed to be done for the children of agricultural labourers, the *dhafa* as they were called, who had either been orphaned or made homeless by the famine. Harold organized a Children's Village for them under the supervision of masters from one of the town schools. The boys lived in groups with a housefather and the girls with a housemother. They were given lessons and they did all the necessary domestic and agricultural work of the village themselves. It was good training and gave the boys and girls the opportunity of education which otherwise they would never have had.

The worst of the famine was over in about six weeks, by which time food supplies sent from the coast to the interior had increased and the R.A.F. was flying regular supplies of grain into the country. The food kitchens were still needed but it was no longer necessary to bring women and children to Mukalla. Relief work had to continue for a long time and the British Government gave £300,000 towards it. Gradually the country returned almost to normal, especially after the rains came, but it was never to be the same again. After the war remittances no longer flowed into the Hadhramaut from Indonesia and Singapore and Hadhramis had to look elsewhere for support, finding it to some extent in Saudi Arabia or one of the other oil-producing countries.

The famine was over, but anyone who has seen a famine-stricken country can never forget it. Where communications are limited it can spread through the land without the town-dwellers being at first aware of what is happening, and when aid is rushed to the worst hit places it takes time for relief to get to all those who need it, and relief is needed at once if the victims are not to die. Tomorrow is a day too late.

Chapter Seventeen

POSTSCRIPT

When the war was nearing its end we were able to leave the Hadhramaut, expecting to return in a few months' time, but it was nearly twenty years before I was to see South Arabia again.

By then there were great changes in Aden, largely due to the enormous increase of British troops and their families which had resulted in many new buildings and improved roads, while the siting of an oil refinery at Little Aden had created an entirely new township there. In other ways also there were tremendous advances. I found Aden girls working in offices, in schools, in broadcasting, and there were two outstanding women's organisations involved with local politics as well as with welfare activities.

Emancipation had not gone as far in the Hadhramaut, although the education of girls had taken great strides in Mukalla where it had reached the stage that Aden had reached twenty years earlier. There was now a secondary girls' school in Mukalla and no one any longer thought it wrong to have his daughter educated, but there were reservations about sending girls abroad for higher education, and purdah was as strict as ever. In the Kathiri State girls' education had only just begun with the opening of the first primary school for girls by the Director of Education in his own house, with his two daughters as the teachers, an almost identical pattern to the start of girls' education in Mukalla when Sheikh Abdulla opened his school for girls with his wife and daughter as teachers.

In spite of local air services, some new roads, developments in agriculture and improved social services, life in the Hadhramaut had hardly changed at all, particularly among the women, except that they now called in the male doctor to attend them at childbirth. Fatima had died and Seiyid

Bubakr Al Kaf had married a young wife to look after him in his old age. Sa'ud, whose wedding I had attended and who was now little more than thirty, was a grandmother; early marriages were still customary and her eldest daughter had been married at fourteen. Seiyid Bubakr's house, where we had spent so much of our time, was now a boys' school, and he lived in a much smaller house on a reduced income. Yet sitting on the floor talking to him with Sa'ud beside me dressed in much the same style as twenty years earlier, it seemed as if all the changes that had taken place in the world outside Wadi Hadhramaut had passed them by, save for the relatively minor inconveniences of fewer servants and less money to spend on gold ornaments.

'Ingrams' Peace' was still being maintained, in spite of occasional disturbances, and the days of chaos and anarchy that we had known in 1934 were barely remembered, a great tribute to Harold's work, which was by no means forgotten. His vision, however, of a country organised by Arabs for Arabs had not developed along the lines he had laid down. There were now a number of 'advisers' in the Hadhramaut and there was an unfortunate division of 'we' (the British) and 'them' (the Arabs), only too reminiscent of the colonial attitude familiar to me in Aden twenty years before.

The political development of South Arabia had been troubling the Colonial Office for some years and by the late fifties it was becoming imperative that something should be done to organise the disparate entities that made up the area into a tidy whole before independence, which, to judge by all the other colonies, was bound to come sooner or later. Federation seemed the obvious way to form an orderly government, but the tidy minds of Whitehall officials have no counterparts in South Arabia, and it was only after considerable financial inducements that one ruler after another in the Western Aden Protectorate joined the Federation. He was then transformed into a Minister, left his carpeted floor in a battlemented fort on a mountain peak for the Federal capital of Al Ittihad near Aden where he was given a house, an exact replica of every other Minister's

L

house, an imposing desk in an office, and usually a British adviser. Any transformation scene in any pantomime was more realistic than the one played out to its inevitable conclusion in South Arabia.

The Qu'aiti Sultan of Shihr and Mukalla and the Kathiri Sultan refused to join the Federation in spite of a great deal of persuasion, because, they said, it was not the wish of their people. It was also thought that oil was going to be found in the northern deserts of the Hadhramaut and no one wished to share the proceeds with all the other states.

I am one of those who feel we should have left South Arabia ten years before we did, for the future of the area was something that had to be worked out by the people themselves and the longer we stayed trying to arrange their future for them the more we confused the situation. Our policy was governed not so much by a wish to help the people of South Arabia as by the idea that we must defend our oil interests in the Gulf, and the base at Aden was part of that strategy. This policy was even more vigorously pursued because of the Bogey Man we had built in the shape of President Gamal Abdul Nasser. Behind every Arab who wanted to be rid of the British we saw Nasser prodding him on, and it was even said that the Egyptian President's aim was to control the oil fields on the other side of the Arabian desert. I have no doubt that President Nasser, like any other Head of State, wants countries to be friendly towards him and would pursue policies to that end, and one of the most attractive to the Arabs that he could pursue in the 1960's was to denounce imperialism or any form of control over Arab territory by a foreign country. Our attack on him in 1956 increased his stature all over the Arab world, and although he was diminished in the eyes of many Arabs when embroiled in the Yemen civil war, they did not see this involvement of Arab against Arab so intolerable as the domination of Arabs by foreigners.

When we were in South Arabia from 1934–44 there was no thought of independence for Aden in the minds of the British nor, for that matter, in the minds of most influential

Arabs who benefited from British orderly government. Self-government within the commonwealth was the goal and the problem was how to fit the Protectorate into this picture. While the two Hadhrami states seemed likely to develop reasonably stable governments, the rest of the Protectorate was as unpredictable as the Scottish clans must have seemed to Queen Elizabeth I.

It is too late to argue what might have happened had we pursued other policies in South Arabia, and when I say that we should have left ten years earlier I am aware that we would have left chaotic conditions behind us; but at least we would not have led the rulers up the garden path with promises of support, which in the end was not forthcoming, and popular leaders whether from Aden or the Protectorate might have had a chance to take over without resorting to the terrorism which killed Arabs and British alike. I am not suggesting that we should have done what the Belgians did in the Congo, but we could have named the day of our departure – perhaps a year in advance – and then have given the opportunity for political parties and tribal chiefs to come to some agreement between themselves without our interference, offering aid for ten years at least, and not taking umbrage if the leaders of the newly independent country also sought help from other western or eastern powers.

It is not just the policy we followed as regards independence that I find regrettable in South Arabia, but also the fact that we did so little over a hundred years to educate and to involve the people in their own government. It is true that the Protectorate offered no return for the money invested in it and this was perhaps a reason, if a mercenary and inhuman one, to leave it alone, but the colony of Aden was necessary to us and we had built it up from almost nothing into a prosperous port, yet there were only a handful of Adenis who held responsible positions. The defence of Aden was in the hands of the British and no Adenis were trained in anything more military than a small force of armed police. Even when the Colonial Office took over from the Government of India and brought ideas of self-government, the

average official had little use for the Adeni Arab, distrusting
the townee with that invariable British dislike for the semi-
educated and romantic fondness for the noble savage. The
fact that there were so many semi-educated Arabs in Aden
only reflected the paucity of the education offered them.

When I returned to the Hadhramaut in 1963 the number
of British living in or around Mukalla filled me with misgiving. Inevitably with the increase in their numbers they
had become isolated from contact with the 'natives'. I was
even told that it was not safe for a European woman to walk
down the main street. I proved this to be the complete
rubbish that I knew it to be, but it only showed how out of
touch the British had become that such a thing could even
be suggested. A few years later it might indeed have been
unsafe, for by then bombs were being thrown by the National
Liberation Front.

In 1963 the Hadhramaut still had high hopes of oil being
found by the Pan-American Oil Company, successors to
Petroleum Concessions which had started exploration in 1937,
when two American geologists stayed with us off and on while
surveying the country by land and from the air. I remember
one of them telling me that oil would never be found in
commercial quantities as there were too many geological
faults, and he seems to have been right for after many
years of search the Pan-American Company gave up a year
or so ago. I am sorry for this as I think that the finding of
oil in desert countries is a satisfactory balance of nature, and
it would have meant a better standard of living for the people
of South Arabia.

It is only too easy to be wise after events and I have to think
hard to remember what I felt about colonialism in the 1930's
knowing how I feel about it now. I think I probably accepted
it as an institution but rebelled against the division between
rulers and ruled; in any case I was brought up to believe it
was the right of people to rule themselves, one of my earliest
recollections as a child was some official function in Newcastle
when, dressed as a colleen, I curtsied to the wife of the guest
of honour and handed over a bouquet with the words 'From

a little Home Ruler'. Certainly by the 1940's I doubted if colonialism was there to stay for I wrote a 'poem' about Africa the last verse of which ran:

Can alien ruler ever come to know
What lies within the heart of those he rules?
Justice, hygiene, and teaching, these he'll sow
In fallow fields. But even though he schools
The outward thought and sees the ripening tree
Fructify and produce enlightened men,
There is hidden mystery he cannot see
In minds of those he yet believes children.
What do their laughter and good manners hide?
The man in bush with all his magic charms,
Or man of learning whose forefathers died
In pagan wars, slave raids and wild alarms.
Do either want white man's paternal hand
Or do they seek to oust him from their land?

The genuine affection and respect of most colonial officials for the people of the country in which they served and their wish to promote their welfare are not to be denied, but paternalism by its very nature denies the right of free expression to the children. When, after the war, nationalism swept round the world like an epidemic, colonial officials had to find ways of explaining this irritant in the colonial oyster shell. It was just the cry of a few demagogues who would do more harm than good if they took control, they said; the masses did not want change, for they appreciated the justice and good order of British administration. The assumption that the 'natives' must prefer the order and justice of our administration to the disorder and injustice of their own was one of the more astonishing aspects of the British attitude towards their colonial subjects. We could not believe that anyone would want us to go. We believed in, and tried to live up to, the ideals of fair play, and our utter confidence in our own righteousness blinded us to the feelings of others. When rudely jolted into the realisation that there were strong forces against us they had to be the forces of Communism or the voices of a minority of semi-educated orators inciting the masses, who would want us to remain if only they could speak for themselves. One after another colonies gained 'freedom' – surely the word was an appalling reflection on the past state of the subject peoples – and yet officials continued to wear blinkers until almost the last moment, especially so in South Arabia where we appeared to be blind to all the signs of opposition to Federation, until we found ourselves once again in a position similar to pre-independent Ireland, India, Kenya or Cyprus. In the end we had to leave the country in the hands of those we had been so confident could never win majority support nor become the leaders of the independent state.

Today South Arabia is called the People's Republic of Southern Yemen and its government hopes that, with the sultans and ruling sheikhs overthrown, the area will remain united under a more popular form of government. Whether this hope is fulfilled or not, one thing is certain – unless oil is one day discovered in commercial quantities, the men and women of South Arabia will have to go on depending on their meagre resources or emigrating to more prosperous countries, as they have done for centuries.

INDEX

Abdulla, Sheikh, teacher and Director of Education Qu'aiti State, starts girls' school, 128, 148; family problems, 129
Abdul Nasser, President Gamal, influence of, 150
Abdul Qadir, second son of Seiyid Hasan Al Bar of Cairo, 106
Abdul Rahman Al Kaf, Seiyid, 15, 17; family of, 20–21
Aden, early history, 1; administration, 2–3; Resident of, 3, 4, 6; Indian influences on, 3; effect of war on, 92; 'streamed' life in, 125; education in, 126, 152; development in, 148
Aden Airways, 77–78
Aden Protectorate, area, 1; tribal states in, 1; administration 2–3; treaties in, 10; bombing in, 45; neglect of, 45–46 (See also Arabia, South)
Agriculture, 6, 38, 40, 42, 47, 48, 52, 139; in Hajr Province, 79, 86–87; in Meifa, 87; in Gheil Ba Wazir, 102; in Yemen, 117, 124
Ahmed Ba Surra, co-Governor of Du'an Province, hospitality of, 37; holds hostages, 98, 99
Ahmed Nasir Al Batati, commander of Qu'aiti State forces, 12–13
Alawi Al Attas, Seiyid, companion on journey up Wadi Amd, respect for father, 47; ambitions of, 48; matrimonial troubles, 48–49; in Wadi Amd, 51–56
Alawiya, Sherifa, a learned woman, 23–25, 62
Alcohol drinking, 73–74
Ali the Bedui, Seiyid, companion on journeys, 54–56, 97
Amd, Wadi, feuds in, 47, 51, 53; description of, 51–55; women in, 50, 52–53, 55; houses in, 52; second visit to, 99–100
Amqan, village in Wadi Rakhia, hospitality in, 140
Arabi Pasha, 109

Arabia, South, change of name, 1, 154; description, 1–2; treaties in, 10; development in, 87, 149–51; federation of, 149–50, 154; independence of, 154
Arabic, learning of, 5, 127
Arabs, character, 2; brotherhood of, 2; individualism of, 2; social divisions among, 4; attitude of British towards, 125 (See also Beduin and Tribes)
Awadh bin Salih, Qu'aiti Sultan, as heir apparent, 12; marital problems, 75–76

Batavia, 91
Beduin, feuds among, 15; protection money demanded by, 16–17; companions on journeys, 33, 35–37, 79–82, 94, 96; childhood of, 80; character, 80; taboos among, 80–81; position of women, 82; explanation of 'beduin', 82; attitude to road building, 131; education of, 133, 145–6
Beit al Faqih, town in Yemen, visit to, 115–16
Besse, Anton, starts air service, 77
Bin Ali, Wadi, journey along, 101–2
Bir Asakir, Hadhrami Beduin Legion fort, 136; garrison in, 139–40, beduin at, 139
Bombing, in South Arabia, 45–46
British, attitude to Arabs in Aden, 125, 127: in Mukalla, 152
British Council, opens club for women in Aden, 126
British Overseas Airways Corporation, connection with Aden Airways, 78
British Broadcasting Corporation, Arabic Service of, 93
Bubakr Al Attas, Seiyid from Hureidha, 47–48; family of, 48–49
Bubakr Al Kaf, Seiyid, C.B.E., 14–15, 17–18; attitude to slaves 21; house of, 22; family of, 23; on educating women, 28; generosity of, 63;